FOREWORD BY

TEENPRENEUR
HOW TO BUILD A
BUSINESS IN YOUR TEENS

ERROL LAWSON

CONTENTS

SECTION 1
DEVELOPING THE ATTITUDE AND MINDSET
OF A SUCCESSFUL ENTREPRENEUR

SECTION 2
CREATING THE BUSINESS AND SHARING IT WITH THE WORLD

ACKNOWLEDGMENTS

I'm grateful to God first and foremost for the grace to be able to get this done inspite of the many challenges that came up along the way. I would like to say a special thanks for all those that contributed to making this book happen. My wife, Kehinde for being a source of strength and encouragement throughout. My team of supporters that provided input, reviews and general encouragement. Ian Spence, Bukebo Dodd, Evans Haim, Daniel Priestley for the Foreward and for blazing a trail for so many of us. Audrey Hayden, Helen May, William Okeyre-Frimpong, Kofi Osei-Kusi, Romannah Malcolm, Helen May, Tina Alton, Jonnie Jensen, Amanda C. Watts, Beverley Burton and Aaron Thomas.

FOREWORD BY DANIEL PRIESTLEY

If you are a teenager and reading this book–congratulations! Regardless of how lucky or unlucky you think you've been in the past, I can tell you that you are perfectly positioned to take advantage of the most exciting times in human history.

In any other period in history, you would have barely had any form of education, healthcare, transport or legal rights. Even in the past 200 years, your destiny would have been to work in a stale, boring factory doing a repetitive job and taking decades to advance from the factory floor to the management room. In the last 100 years, the most exciting and important work for normal people was to join the military and fight in a war. All the money stayed inside the circles of elite families and there was no hope of a regular person building any wealth in their lifetime.

Today you are living in a time where there are self made millionaires in their 20s who started with nothing. There are teenagers who sell products online to customers all over the world. At the age of just 15, some have millions of people watching their YouTube videos and following them on Instagram.

You are the perfect age because you're young and free in a world where many things are possible that have never been possible before. You can answer any question simply by Googling, you can travel cheaply on discount airlines and couch-surf your way around the world. You can connect with friends all over the globe and share ideas and resources, and all from your phone.

Every song is yours to listen to, every film is ready to watch, every idea is ready to be shared, every person is available to meet. There is also more money available than every before, and all the time it's moving around you at the speed of light. All you need is to become a little bit entrepreneurial, solve problems for people, add value to the world and get creative; if you do, the rewards are endless. You'll end up old and wrinkly one day but you'll be so happy that you lived a life worth bragging about.

It's easy to think sometimes that life is hard, that you're not as lucky as some people or that you'd be better off if things were easier. It's an illusion, you've hit the jackpot and everyone older than you knows it. Anyone over the age of 30 would trade in everything they own to be in your shoes right now—young, curious, adventurous and full of potential.

This book is going to help you to unlock some of that potential and to build a life that you are in love with.

I wish you all the best on your journey.

—Daniel Priestley

Best Selling Author of 'How to become a Key person of influence', 'The Entrepreneur Revolution' and 'Oversubscribed'.

ABOUT THE AUTHOR

Errol Lawson is the Co–Founder of Emerge Leadership UK and Ghana. He faced and overcame several challenges in his teenage years and has become an author, entrepreneur and motivational speaker. Errol writes about the challenges faced in his teens in his first book entitled "From the Postcode to the Globe–How to overcome limitations and realise your potential"

Errol and the team at Emerge specialise in helping schools to create outstanding cultures. They do this by providing powerful motivational talks and workshops that help increase student engagement and their motivation about their education. They have worked with thousands of young people, across the UK and Ghana. Errol is also the senior leader of Bridge Point Church, based in Birmingham UK. You can find out more about Errol by visiting his website www.errollawson.com

> "......My thanks go to you for your inspirational speech and imparting your wisdom to our students .....and staff, in a lively, engaging and personalised way! I have received lots of positive feedback from our students."
>
> —Julie Anderson,
> Deputy Head, Moseley School, Birmingham

> "Your heart/mission and values are really clear. You have an important role to play in enabling leaders at all levels

to realise their potential and how character defines leaders (and their organisations!)"

—S. Elsear Samworth Ent. Academy

"I was at a position in my career where I needed some guidance and confidence in bringing back my "believe it you can do it!" attitude, Errol was able to quickly identify what type of coaching I needed and focussed me clearly on aspects of my own confidence that had been hidden away for a while. I strongly recommend a coaching session with Errol for people eager to evolve to a higher level of personal confidence and professional satisfaction"

—Nisha Vaitha,
Assistant Head, Golden Hillock School

Services for Schools:

Based on the book Teenpreneur - How to build a business in your teens, Teenpreneur talks and workshops are focused on enhancing business acumen. Whilst giving teens an opportunity to learn the ABCs of entrepreneurship and apply those techniques to craft a viable business plan. With veteran entrepreneurs to serve as instructors, we guarantee an enriching, motivating experience that will help transform young minds into major players.

We offer:

- Extended motivational school assemblies
- Half day workshops
- Full day enterprise challenge events for a whole year group

Teenpreneurs will:

- Get an understanding of the world of business
- Learn how other teens have succeeded in business and ho they can do the same
- Understand how to save and invest wisely
- Develop strong leadership and team working skills
- Build their confidence
- Learn from successful entrepreneurs, and corporate professionals
- Take part in interactive challenges that will develop their business skills
- Develop and practice presentation skills

Email: errol@errollawson.com Web: www.errollawson.com /
www.emerge-leadership.com
Twitter @errollawson

Introduction

Firstly, I want to congratulate you for taking the time to read this book. It's quite likely that if you're reading this book, you are already excited at the prospect of creating and running your own business at some point in the future. Perhaps you have an idea in your head that you are thinking about or have already started developing. Perhaps you would like to start your own business but you have no idea where to start. This book is definitely going to be a step in the right direction for you.

How did Teenpreneur come about?

We began to develop the Teenpreneur concept in the UK in 2013. The term 'Teenpreneur' was inspired by what I saw Albert and Comfort Ocran doing in Ghana with their 'Teenpreneurship' project. For a number of years they have been developing the entrepreneurial skills of teenagers in Ghana, something we felt was missing in the UK, especially within inner-city communities.

In the US there is another inspirational "Teenpreneur" platform that is hosted by 'Black Enterprise' which is also doing amazing things to inspire and train our youth.

As we looked more into the idea of helping teenagers to develop their entrepreneurial mindsets we began to come across studies that suggested more than 50% of teens today were thinking of starting their own business at some point in time. I recently read a report by Unltd that said more than 50% of young people today are considering creating their own business rather than pursuing the traditional career path.

The reason there are so many young people today thinking of going into business is partly because of the global popularisation of 'entrepreneurship'. Programmes like 'The Apprentice', 'Shark Tank' and 'Dragons Den' have made entrepreneurship more attractive and given more people confidence to believe it is something they too can do.

The 50% figure is also an indication of the shift in the social consciousness around success and money. For many years schools taught that academic success is the only way to true wealth and prosperity. They proclaimed that if you didn't get the grades, you were going to be on the scrap heap of life and amount to little. Because of the changes in the global economy, there are people all over the world with degrees coming out of their ears, but who are finding it very difficult to get a job. The traditional system has not worked for them.

In this book I advocate a more complete form of education–self-education. This is what you teach yourself or choose to learn outside of the classroom. Its what you learn by actually creating something or by spending time working with, or for, a successful person, and being mentored by them.

My view is that you should do your best in school, work hard. The discipline of education will serve you well later in life. However, the skills or knowledge you take it upon yourself to learn in your own time are what will eventually set you apart from the rest. Whether it comes through reading books, attending events or spending time with mentors. Your self-education is going to be the key to your success.

The biggest hurdles or obstacles that young people share with me about starting a business are:

a) A lack of motivation

b) Not knowing where to start

c) Fear, and

d) Raising the money to get started

I'm going to address each of these factors in the book. In this book I want to help you to see to that:

a) You can start a business at any time in your life and I'll show you how you can get started

b) You can discover and develop new ideas

c) To be a business owner is fun and its a respectable decision to make

d) To make money legitimately is good and show you how you can raise the money to get started.

e) That you don't need to be an old person to start a business, you can start now.

f) That you have what it takes to start and succeed in business

Have a pen and paper ready and be prepared to take action. In the chapters of this book I will share lessons and stories from my own life as well as those of other individuals that have inspired me and I hope will inspire you. These are Individuals who have truly MADE IT HAPPEN.

This is your time

There is only one thing you need to know and that is that YOU CAN LEARN ANYTHING. There has never been a time in all of human history when there has been so much opportunity available to us all. Breakthroughs in technology have made it possible for us to access information on any given subject at the click of a button.

The internet is the biggest opportunity we all have in our hands right now. If you so choose, and are willing to put in the hard work and dedication, you can learn how to do anything. And, of course, you can learn how to build a successful business, even as a teenager or young adult.

The unique advantage that you and I have at this moment in history, is that everybody and almost anybody is connected via the internet. Before the internet you would often hear people say that you are no more than two people away from anyone else in the world. This was called the "6 degrees of separation". I would argue that in this day and age you are no more than a few clicks of your mouse away from any one individual. Via LinkedIn, Twitter, Facebook and other social platforms, we can connect with almost anybody.

The internet along with mobile phone technology has broken down the barriers of communication and made it possible for us to reach people all over the world, on different continents, living in different time zones. People who share the same ideas. hopes and dreams. Rather than merely thinking of ourselves as local citizens, with local issues and challenges and opportunities, more and more people are beginning to see that actually we are living in a bigger pond. We truly are a part of a global community and opportunities are in every part of the world.

I had my first job at age 15 working on a market with my uncle. Although I was going out on a Saturday morning, helping to set up the stall and working all day, I didn't fully appreciate the opportunity. I was there in person but I didn't truly believe that running a business was something that I could actually do myself because I didn't know how. I didn't understand how someone got an idea or business off the ground and I was never shown how. At age 19 someone showed me how and I was able to get started. My hope is that by the time you get to the end of this book you will be able to see exactly how you can get started and succeed in business, even at a young age.

The book is divided into two sections:

Section A: **Behind the scenes.** Developing the Mindset and attitude of an entrepreneur

Section B: **Showtime.** Creating the business and sharing it with the world

In Section A you will learn:

- How successful entrepreneurs think about money vs How unsuccessful entrepreneurs think about money.

- How to hustle like a pro and become the business person you really want to be

- How to beat fear and develop the self-belief and confidence you need to succeed

- How to develop your public speaking and communication skills and be able to speak to anyone, anytime, anywhere.

- How to build a support network of individuals that will help to get you from where you are to where you want to be

- How to overcome challenges, handle pressure and develop the courage to win in business

In section B you will:

- Learn how to raise the money you need to get your idea off the ground

- Learn how to take an idea from conception to implementation

- Create your own online business in 7 simple steps

- Understand how to market your product in a way that will boost your audience from just your friends and family to hundreds of people in just 7 days

If you are new to the idea of being an entrepreneur or have never had any exposure to business, I would recommend you start with section A. If you have a good understanding about what it takes to get started in business and you just want to get an idea of how to take a business or idea online and how to promote it, you might want to go to section B. The best idea is to read the whole thing, all the way through. Have a pen and paper at the side as you read to take notes.

ACCESS GRANTED

Consider this book your blueprint, a guide book, the access key that you need to get that project, business or idea off the ground. I want to leave you with absolutely no excuse for not getting started AND making a profit right now. Here's to your success!

I look forward to hearing your stories of success. Please email me at errol@errollawson.com with your stories.

Section 1

Developing the Attitude and Mindset of a Successful Entrepreneur

CHAPTER 1

Learn how to hustle like a pro

"Good things happen to those who hustle."

—**Anaïs Nin**

What causes people to quit on themselves and their ideas? What stops people that have so much potential and ability from completing what they started?

I honestly couldn't tell you how many times I have felt like giving up on this entrepreneurial journey. Times when I've felt like chucking it in and getting a job again. When family or friends have tried to tell me that, maybe I should do something else. It's been really challenging, but something inside me just believes that it's possible. That there is something greater for me to do or be a part of, that success is possible. I refuse to quit.

I remember times when I would get to the end of the month and not have enough money to pay my rent and my bills. And worse still, I had no guarantee of income for the next two months either! Talk about being in a tough situation. I had nowhere to go. I even started looking at job adverts and thinking this entrepreneurial path is not for me. In those types of situations you really need to have some good people around you, you have to be resilient, and you have to be able to hustle.

COMMIT TO YOUR GOALS AND DREAMS

To commit to achieving or realising our goals and dreams is to go after them come what may; through trials and storms, through challenges and tests. It means to keep going even when the crowd is telling you you're not good enough or you're not going to make it. That's what real commitment is. It's staying and seeing the job through when you feel like giving up.

For a great many entrepreneurs, students and business owners the very thing they are afraid of is success. Due to this fear they unintentionally sabotage themselves because they believe that they will be seen as a fraud, or that they're not good enough. It's not easy to stand up in front of your community or your peers and say, here I am, the expert, I know what I'm talking about". It's hard because it opens us up to criticism and many people fear rejection. And secondly, because we know that we will have to constantly perform in those areas for the rest of our life in order to maintain the status.

In such cases, the challenge is for us to overcome this fear by shouting the loudest about the good work we do. If we have done or created something that is worth talking about, that adds value to the lives of others we ought to talk to people about it. We ought to share it with the world. There's a verse in the Bible that says "let your light so shine before men that your father in heaven may see your good works and be glorified." I love that. If you've got something good to say, say it loud and say it proud.

One of the great joys in life is being able to complete something. To see it through to the end of its life cycle, overcoming whatever challenges come along the way. There are always going to be times when we feel like quitting or throwing in the towel, but we have to be men and women of conviction. Who will stand for what we believe. I don't mean inflexible concrete towers, rather individuals that are able to be flexible and adapt to the situation and always willing to learn and grow, whilst being committed to the end goal.

I know I make it sound kind of straightforward when actually it can be quite hard to do. It can be hard because today there are so many distractions that look like good opportunities. So many things vying for our attention, temptation if you like, is everywhere. You need to "remain true to who you are and your word", when all around there are appealing and tantalising desires beckoning. This is why you have to really know why you are doing what you have set out to do.

KNOW YOUR 'WHY'

In the last 12 months I have had the chance to work with some amazing young people in more than 50 schools around the UK. The biggest challenge that young people in the UK seem to struggle with is apathy. Apathy is basically being indifferent about life. When young people get apathetic unfortunately they give up easily when challenges come their way. Whats the cure for apathy? its having a sense of meaning or purpose. Its knowing WHY you are here and WHY you are doing what you are doing.

It is possible to achieve your goals. In fact, if we are going to succeed and achieve our goals and dreams in life, we have to use the challenges that come as opportunities for us to grow and become better people. We have to realise that these things that come our way to distract us are sent to test our focus and commitment. I've found that the stronger and clearer I am about my purpose and my 'why', the more able I am to commit to any given task.

Your WHY is your reason for even attempting to achieve the goal you have set yourself. It's the thing that motivates you to keep going. Everyone's WHY is personal to them. Having a really strong and clear reason 'why' will give you the extra motivation you often need to keep going.

I'm a big boxing fan. There is a world famous boxer named Bernard Hopkins. You may not have heard of him but he is a legend in the world of boxing. He was asked by an interviewer what his 'WHY' was and, "What makes you keep fighting at the highest level at age 55?" He said "The mindset that I have before I go into a fight is that the refrigerator at home is empty." "That's a strong mindset that you must have when the reality is the refrigerator is empty and you got to win the fight to keep it full," said Hopkins. He went on to say, "Now if you are blessed and you are talented enough and get the right breaks and your refrigerator now becomes full, you keep that same mentality that it's empty, even though it's full." It was this reference point that Hopkins used to keep him focussed whilst being in the ring with some of the best fighters in the world.

Another example from boxing for you. Hopefully, you will have heard of Floyd 'Money' Mayweather. He is probably one the greatest professional boxers and sportsmen of all time. At the time of writing this book to you Floyd has gone a record breaking 50 fights without being defeated. Making him the highest paid sportsman in the world. His record is amazing. You should go and check him out on Youtube, if you've not come across him.

I mention Floyd because one of the mottos he is famous for is "Hard Work and Dedication!". This is what has been the key to his success. In each of his gym training sessions you will hear him shout out "Hard work!" and his trainers and the other fighters training in his gym will shout out in chorus "Dedication!" "Hard Work!"–"Dedication!" Here are a couple of quotes from Floyd himself:

> "I come from a very rough background, and I'm saying that if you work hard and dedicate yourself that you can make it, too."
>
> **—Floyd Mayweather**

> "You know, as a young child, I lay in my bedroom and I swore to myself then: 'I'm not going to smoke and I'm not going to drink.' And I said I'm not going to just say that when I'm a kid. I'm going to stick to that as an adult. I kept that in mind my whole life."
>
> **—Floyd Mayweather**

"Well, you've got certain obstacles that get in your way throughout your career, but you have to be a strong individual."

—Floyd Mayweather

Becoming a successful entrepreneur or business owner is hard work. There are no two ways about it. Get it into your head from the very beginning that achieving your goals is not going to be easy. If you accept this from the start of your journey, you will be better prepared mentally when the tough times come. If it was easy everyone would be doing it. There is absolutely nothing wrong with putting the necessary hard work in now, knowing that you might reap the rewards later. In actual fact, most successful entrepreneurs have prepared themselves to work and live like nobody else for a few years, because they believe that in a few years from now they will truly live like nobody else, when their goals have begun to be realised.

The obstacles are always going to be there; the naysayers are always going to be there. There will always be some kind of spanner in the works, but to experience the richness and fullness of life, we need to be able to commit.

None of us are perfect; nor will we be in this lifetime. We have to be willing to take a risk and trust that we will learn along the way. When a spaceship sets off, on its course from the space station, heading towards its intended destination, it spends the majority of the journey off course. Constantly going back and forth, contending with the atmospheric elements until it eventually safely arrives at its port of call. Our lives are very similar.

Case study: Ayla Hutchinson, 15

Ayla Hutchinson, 15, of Taranaki, New Zealand, has invented and patented the Kindling Cracker, made a profitable business out of it with the help of her parents, and improved the lives of countless people around the world. The Kindling Cracker has a fairly self-explanatory name. It is a tool that cuts kindling (chips of wood for fire starting) safely without having to swing a sharp instrument past your fingers. Ayla invented it after seeing her mum injure her hand when using a tomahawk to cut kindling.

Don't be too hard on yourself for the times you get it wrong. Learn to pick yourself up and go again. Get back on track. The mistakes that we make provide us with the experience and lessons we need to be able to do it better next time around.

A good way to help you to commit to your goals or objectives is to have some kind of accountability group or support structure in place that will help you to stay on task. It's important that the people that you spend most of your time with are like-minded individuals that share your values. These types of relationships have accountability naturally built into them. They will naturally challenge you to stay on track.

What do I mean by accountability? I like this definition: "The obligation of an individual or organisation to account for its activities, accept responsibility for them, and to disclose the results in a transparent manner. It also includes the responsibility for money or other entrusted property."

By making yourself accountable to others, you help to ensure growth, progress and success.

To take your accountability and personal development a step further, you can start what's called a Mastermind group. A Mastermind is a group of 3-12 people that is intentionally created to provide support for each other and hold each other accountable to personal or business goals. Mastermind groups can meet up as regularly as is convenient for the group members. For example, on a weekly, fortnightly or monthly basis. Every group is different. Some meet in person, some might meet over Skype. These groups provide great accountability and opportunity for growth. (To find out more about Mastermind groups, please read "Think and Grow Rich" or "The Laws of Success", by Napoleon Hill or do a Google search for Mastermind groups.)

It's important to have the right people in your Mastermind group. I created my first group when I was about 20 years old. I'd read about the power of Masterminds in "The Laws of Success". I followed the outline in the book to the 'T'. I got around 12 friends together who were quite successful and well established in their businesses. My challenge was that I had some very strong personalities in that group that I didn't have the skills to be able to manage effectively. . At that stage, I didn't have the required leadership skills.

I learned lots from the experience and built my self-confidence, just from stepping out of my comfort zone and trying it out. Unfortunately, it didn't last very long because I hadn't prepared effectively. I find that the more prepared I am the more confident I am. If the people you have in mind are successful confident people make sure you prepare well and make it worth their while. I learned from the experience and started another such group which is now running successfully and helping all of the members to grow their businesses.

It's about having a mindset and attitude of continual growth and development. Anyone can say all the right stuff, but are they living it day to day? Do they have a routine built into their daily practice that will help them to succeed and achieve their goals and dreams? You've got to believe that successful people do certain things that make them successful. It doesn't just happen.

Someone with a growth-mindset doesn't make excuses about their lack of education or opportunities, or about the disadvantages of their upbringing. They care not for statistics that tell them success is not possible for them. They diligently and tenaciously commit to their own process of self education. Reading and consuming all the information they can that will help them to grow. Seeking out the mentorship and advice that will help them to arrive at their destination.

IF I CAN DO IT, YOU CAN DO IT TOO

I just about made it through school, getting my GCSE's. However, I dropped out of college and didn't get my 'A levels' or go to university straight away. It wasn't until many years later that I applied to study at a university. And what got me in wasn't my academic results, it was my life experience. In my pursuit of personal growth and development I came across the writings of people like Ralph Waldo Emerson and others, who spoke about the importance of self-education. I realised that if I was going to wait for the system to educate me on who I was, what my potential was and what I was capable of achieving, I would be waiting for ever. I saw more clearly that the education system, although it has its benefits was actually, in my opinion, an exam factory designed to churn out individuals that would further enhance the 'system'. A system I didn't fit into. It wasn't designed to help us realise our God-given potential.

I decided I was going to take responsibility for my own learning. I began to read. I started by asking myself which skills I needed to develop. I read books written by experts in those areas and began to educate myself. The likes of Emerson and others were right, I could educate myself to success. I sought out mentors in the fields in which I wanted to develop and they very generously offered me guidance and support.

My friend, you can do the same. Change begins with you. You can decide today that your past doesn't determine your future. You can choose to educate yourself. To seek out the support, the books or information that is needed to help you to turn your life around or accelerate your life to the next level. Ask yourself right now, "Have I been consistent in taking the opportunities that have been offered to me?""Am I truly committed to my own growth and development?"

NO MORE EXCUSES

I've worked inside prisons and met several prisoners, serving life or indefinite sentences, that have chosen to study university courses online while they are in prison in order to maximise their time and come out of jail with the skills to live a different life. In the world that we live in today, there really can be no excuse for not making something of our lives. Information is in abundance. The 'playing field' probably more level than it has been in all of human history.

Whether it's through the internet, mobile technology, television, or other media, everyone is competing for our attention. We have got to be more deliberate about what we give our time to and for how long. We need to give our time only to those things that are going to help us grow towards our highest priorities. You've got to shake yourself up and start telling yourself "ANYTHING IS POSSIBLE!"

Obviously, it can be really hard to commit when you feel as though you're not sure exactly where you're going. This is why having goals and a personal vision for your future is so important. You've got to **decide** where you are going. As a teenager and young adult I really felt as though I had nothing to live for or nothing worth committing to. That was largely because of a sense of low self-worth. Not believing that I deserved the best. Growing up in a single parent family, getting involved with the wrong crowd. Not feeling validated or recognised for who I was as a person. All these things compounded to making me a very insecure and unfulfilled person.

For any of us to change this we need something bigger to commit to. A bigger vision or picture of the future that can guide us and pull us up out of the position that we are in. A set of inspiring goals that will motivate us and encourage us to keep going.

For me, like many others, my vision came in a variety of ways. To be honest, knowing that I am liked and loved by God has helped me to like and love myself and in turn to like and love others. That motivated me and gave me immense courage. I think it was Donald Trump that said, "If you're going to think, think big!"

Everyday we see or meet people, men and women, young and old, black and white from around the world that are settling for less than they deserve. Sometimes this is because of events which were beyond their control. Situations that crushed their confidence and self-belief, and now their lives repeat in negative cycles they feel ill-equipped to break.

I know that for some teenagers or young people it's really difficult to look into the future. My question to you is, have you tried? Have you actually taken the time to sit down for a while, somewhere relaxed and quiet to think about the type of future that you want to have? I really want to encourage you to give it a try. When you search for and find a vision and purpose for your life, the clouds will clear.

You may have to let go of some of the negative people and things that you have in your environment that are holding you back. Things that remind you of your past. Instead, you'll need to surround yourself with positive people and things that will remind you of your potential and where you're heading in life.

CHOOSE THE RIGHT FRIENDS

I had no idea at the beginning of this journey how lonely the entrepreneurial path I was about to embark on was going to be. I had grown up with many friends. I was quite popular amongst my friends and in my community. I initially found it very difficult to deal with the lack of support and encouragement that I received from some of best friends; people that I had grown up with all of my life.

I don't know whether they doubted whether I would be able to do what I was setting out to achieve. I don't know whether they were so consumed in their own life challenges that my work and my dreams was just of no concern to them. I wonder whether I had just surprised them with the talk of business success and they had no idea how to support me. However, the support from the friends I grew up with, that I hoped at the time would come, failed to materialise.

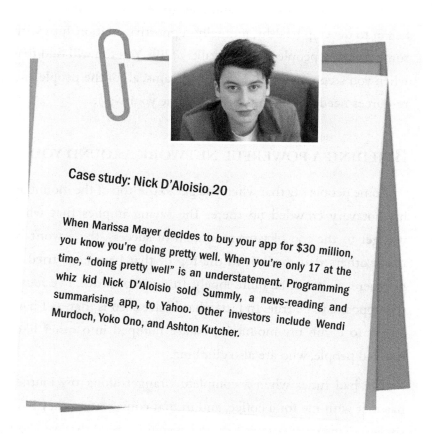

Case study: Nick D'Aloisio, 20

When Marissa Mayer decides to buy your app for $30 million, you know you're doing pretty well. When you're only 17 at the time, "doing pretty well" is an understatement. Programming whiz kid Nick D'Aloisio sold Summly, a news-reading and summarising app, to Yahoo. Other investors include Wendi Murdoch, Yoko Ono, and Ashton Kutcher.

This was an important lesson for me to learn. If I was going to achieve anything of great recognition I wouldn't be able to rely on the same support structures or mindsets that had gotten me this far. I was going to have to break the mould and step outside of my comfort zone. I wasn't about to let the lack of support stop me. I was passionate about what I was doing, and with or without them, as far I was concerned, I was going to make it happen.

It was amazing that as I began to pursue this vision, I began to meet like-minded people . People I'd never met or heard of before. People that were passionate and committed to the same cause. I began to develop healthy, mutually supportive relationships with some amazing people from all walks of life. You too will find that when you step out and follow your dreams, all of the people and resources needed will, in time, also come your way .

BUILDING A POWERFUL NETWORK AROUND YOU

Some people say that when you get to the 'top of the mountain' it's not very crowded up there. The saying implies that when you get to the top of your mountain of success, there won't be many others that made it to the top or that have even tried to get there, so it will be quite lonely. In my experience, I've found the opposite to be true. In fact, what I have seen is that, as I have begun to climb my mountain, I have bumped into other like-minded people, who are also climbing.

I've had times when a complete stranger along my journey has met with me for a coffee, and in that conversation they have spoken to me words of wisdom and encouragement that were just what I needed to hear. I have also had opportunities to do the same for others . . As you go after your dream, you are going to meet lots and lots of new people. Your network is going to expand; you are going to grow from strength to strength. As you develop your ability to harness and manage these new relationships and opportunities that come your way, you will increase your chances of success.

There's a great verse in the Bible that says, "A man who wants friends must show himself friendly," Proverbs 18:24

In other words, over time you have to be able to become someone that is able to speak to and build relationships with people from all walks of life, even complete strangers . There are going to be times when you're going to need to be able to stand up before a crowd, or large audience and share your ideas, and talk about your business. I'll talk more about communication and public speaking later.

The point I want to make here is that you need to start to recognise that there are people out there in the big wide-world that have ideas, resources, connections and personal stories, that can help you to move your business ideas closer to reality. How you find these people, connect with them and build relationships, is a skill you must develop. Let me give you a few tips that have helped me to build a large network over the last few years.

KEYS TO EFFECTIVE NETWORKING
PERSON TO PERSON

1. We're all equal

It is important to realise that their are different levels of success. If someone has achieved a certain level of success in a field they deserved to be respected for that. However, avoid getting caught in the trap of behaving like you're a fan of the person. Don't get caught up in 'idol worship'. That person is a human being just like you. They maybe successful, but they too have made mistakes, they bleed, they need oxygen to stay alive, they are human. So don't be intimidated by other people. Be respectful but not afraid. Make up your mind in advance that you refuse to be intimidated by anyone you meet at a networkingtype event. Always be respectful but never be intimidated.

2. Win Win

Always think win-win. To think win-win means to guarantee a favourable outcome for everyone involved. Always be prepared to give back, to serve others, to offer your services the same way someone has been kind enough to offer theirs. When it comes to networking, some people behave like parasites. They go to meetings and take, take, take. All they're concerned for is what they can get and people see them coming a mile off and run. Be careful not to become like these kinds of people.

3. Ask questions and then shut up

When you meet someone, don't talk over them, don't get distracted by other things happening around the room. Do your best to give the person you are speaking to your complete attention. You don't need to do all the talking. In fact, the best thing you can do is ask a few open ended questions and let them speak while you listen attentively. From their responses to your questions you will begin to establish whether there are any grounds here to develop a mutually beneficial relationship. If there isn't, that's ok. Just say, "Nice to meet you" and move on. If you do sense a connection, you can develop the relationship further.

4. Keep it real

Don't pretend, don't fake it, don't try and be what you're not. I meet some people and they' try to show that they are the newest, biggest and best thing in town, when, in actual fact, they haven't really done anything of significance. The right people that you're meant to meet and connect with are out there. Either you will find them, or they will find you. All you need to do is be consistent, be real, and be open to meeting new people and making new connections. You don't need to force the issue or even be witty about it. Just be consistent and be open. The goal is to be so good at what you do that people begin to talk about you, and you go from being the one who pursues other people for help, to the one who is being pursued. People are now seeking you out to help, or use your services or products.

5. Business cards not essential

In this world of technology, business cards are no longer a necessity. You can simply take your phone out, save someone's number, take down their email address and website details, and store them in a contact in your phone. If you have a database or CRM for all of your contacts, you can probably transfer them straight from your phone into your database. Don't get hung up on business cards. They have a place but they are not essential.

6. Be in the right place at the right time

I heard of a woman once who was studying to be a lawyer. She had been speaking to her mother about marriage and the type of man that she wanted to marry. She decided that she wanted to marry a doctor. Doctors were thought of as stable guys, earning good money and to be able to provide security for the family. So with her goal in mind, she chose not to do her study on campus in the library where her friends were studying law . Instead, she made her way over to the library where the doctors studied. In time, she made friends with many doctors. Eventually, one approached her and asked her on a date. Many years later, they married. I call that successful networking–positioning yourself in the place of maximum opportunity. Do some research to find out where the events are taking place in your area or country and get to the right places. Don't waste your time trying to meet new people in places where you won't find the people you need to meet.

KEYS TO EFFECTIVE BUSINESS
NETWORKING ONLINE

I asked my friend Jonnie Jensen who is a Social Media Expert who helps individuals and businesses to enhance their online presence, to give you a few tips for effective networking online.

By Jonnie Jensen, Founder, Live and Social, *www.liveandsocial. com*

Understanding and using social media effectively can be a huge asset at the start of your business. Just like face to face networking, you need to know what you are talking about, be talking to the right people and do it regularly so that people get to know you.

I like to break this down as Content, Contacts and Conversation.

Firstly Content. You need to decide what you want to talk about and be known for. On the internet this is how people – and indeed Google – will find you and decide if you are worth talking to. Think not only about what you want to talk about work out what your target audience needs to know to be more successful. If you can become known as someone who provides this information, then people will seek you out. You may even become known as an 'Influencer' on those subjects. Decide on three or five themes you will create content on. In terms of finding and sharing other people's content, add another three or four topics which are relevant but which you are not an expert on yourself. By creating and sharing content in this planned out way, you will find and attract your target audience.

Second up is Contacts. You need to find the right people to network and talk to. On social networks, people's profiles, bio and the content they share will help you identify them. Make a list of the kind of people you want to connect with. Think about their job title, skills, interests, location and keywords that relate to their work. You can then use these words to do searches on social networks, or dedicated search tools, such as icerocket, socialmention or followerwonk.

When you reach out to connect with people, make sure you do so in an open and generous manner. Make sure they can see you have researched them properly and then suggest ways in which you could help each other before trying to sell something.

And finally, Conversation. Just like a networking event or making friends in a new town, you need to see people on a regular basis to form a relationship. Your relationships with other business owners and people in your industry are important because they will either buy from you or recommend you to others.

On social networks it is important to focus on Influencers. These are people who put out regular content and have a good number of followers. You can check to see who these people are by their Klout.com score. Put these people in Twitter lists, Facebook contact groups, Google Plus circles and tag them on LinkedIn, so that you can focus on them. Share and comment on their content. Be part of their community and you will soon be able to call them part of yours. Follow the same process with your prospects. Be interested in them, share their content and as you do so they will be drawn closer to choosing to work with or buy from you.

An important thing to remember in all of this is to be consistent and authentic. Personality is important as you want people to feel like they are getting to know you. Be prepared to share from your personal interests when appropriate. It is no different to deals being done on the golf course. We might be doing it online but it's not called social media for nothing – so be sociable!

ACTION:

---

1. **As you begin on your journey as an entrepreneur, challenging times will come that will make you feel like quitting, these are the times you need to have some good people around you that can encourage you on. You have to be resilient and make to most of opportunities.**

Look around you at your family, friends, those people you know or know of and ask yourself?

A. The network I need to maximise

- Who encourages me?
- Who believes in me?
- Who challenges me to dream think big?
- Who supports and challenges me to improve?
- Who can help me?
- How can I get more of their influence in my life?

B The network I need to minimise

- Who limits me?
- Who presents barriers rather than solutions?

- How can you minimise their impact in your life?

- (That doesn't mean fall out with family and friends – just mentally distance your self from people holding you back)

2. **Having a bigger vision or a bigger picture of the future is very important if you want to be successful in life. It is difficult to be committed when you are not sure of where you are going. You have to decide on where you are going and what you want to achieve for yourself. To be able to overcome challenges you have to understand your WHY. Having a sense of meaning or purpose is also a cure for apathy.**

'GOALS + PASSION = DETERMINATION.' Beverley Burton

- Decide what you're passionate about.

- Decide what you really want to achieve.

- Why do you want to do this?

- What will your life look and feel like when you've achieved your goals?

- Who will this help?

(There are free goal setting tools in the equipped2succeed Learning Tools section of beverleyburton.com)

3. **If becoming successful is an easy thing, everybody would be successful. Becoming successful as an entrepreneur or business owner is total hard work and dedication.**

- Decide what you're prepared to pay in time, energy and effort.
- What are you prepared to do to reach your goals?
- What are you prepared to sacrifice to achieve your goals?
- How many hours a week are you going to work on this?

PLAN – DO – REVIEW (Fail to plan – plan to fail.)

Successful entrepreneurs are not paralysed by planning – plans are used to ensure **FOCUS – You are focused – Your action is focused.**

Winners constantly review:

- What did I want to happen?
- What actually happened?
- What's the gap?
- What am I going to do about it?

4. **Achieving your goals requires commitment and commitment is not possible without proper accountability. Having a support group that you can be accountable helps you to stay focused, true and committed to your goals.**

Use your answers to 1 A. above to form an informal group or more formal 'Advisory Board' – a few volunteers who bring different, relevant skills and experience and want to help you. Holding focused meetings with them will help you to progress. Use similar agenda items each time – you report on things like:

- What I have done since the last meeting.

- Where I am now.

- Things that have gone well

- Challenges

- Next priorities.

Board members – challenge, support and advise you.

Going through this process will help you to accurately reflect, focus and plan and ultimately get things done – bringing together the best advice at your disposal

This is also the sort of process that can help you get used to dealing with more formal company boards.

5. Master the keys to effective networking.

As you begin to pursue your dreams and goals, you are going to meet people and your network is going to expand. Developing your abilities to harness and manage these relationships and opportunities that come your way will increase your chances of success.

- Find groups and individuals who are in your field of endeavour – in the relevant on-line community of interest and in your local community.

- Make a Contribution – to discussions, to forum, ask question, offer help etc.

- Find out what's working for others in your field and learn from them.

- Make sure you can tell people you do and what you want to achieve – simply and succinctly, whilst allowing your passion to shine through. Practice this with family, friends, mentors, your 'board etc.

"A man who wants friends must show himself friendly" Proverbs 18: 24

There are people out there with ideas, resources, connections and personal stories that can help you move your business ideas closer to reality.

'You can get whatever you want in life as long as you help enough other people get what they want' Zig Ziglar

CHAPTER 2

Get the right money mindset

"If a person gets his attitude toward money straight, it will help straighten out almost every other area of his life".

—Billy Graham

If you haven't faced it yet, you're likely to be challenged by it at some point in life—the wrong attitude towards money. Unfortunately, a lot of people seem to have it. I confess, I had the wrong attitude towards money for a long time too. Like many others, I was double-minded. I believed, on one hand, that money was a necessity, a good thing that could solve problems, and on the other hand, I believed that money was "the root of all evil". I believed that money was something that would make me a bad person and having to much of it would corrupt me. Can you see the conflict here?

The problem is, when anyone holds two conflicting beliefs in their head so strongly they actually go into a state of paralysis, taking no action at all and end up ruining their chances.

As you are about to embark upon this new business venture, it is important that you do so with a healthy attitude towards money. It will make life a lot easier for you. So here are a few things for you to consider.

1. Money is neutral

Money is like a knife. The knife itself isn't dangerous; the one who is holding it is. Money, in and of itself, is neither good nor bad. It's neutral. Neither does money make you good or bad. People will do a lot of immoral or illegal things to get money. This usually happens when the love of money has consumed a person so much that they begin to forget right from wrong, lose their conscience and start to use money to do bad rather than good. Money isn't to blame though. Money only magnifies who you are in your life. If someone gets a lot of money and goes and does bad stuff, that impulse was already in them.

Having the money didn't change them, it brought out what was already there, in the same way that if someone gets a lot of money and does good things, the good was already there too. Money itself isn't necessarily the problem. The problem lies in the heart or motives of the individual that has the money.

Money is a form of currency. Currency comes from the word 'currere', meaning 'to flow to'. Where your money will flow to is your choice. Don't blame the money. Money will only amplify who you really are.

To my mind, money is a good thing. It solves problems, enables me to develop the work that I do, impact more lives and generally be of greater service to God and humanity. There are lots of examples of corrupt, rich people, but there are also many, many examples of rich, moral people.

2. Money follows service (and hard work)

In order to get paid and earn money you need to provide a service or create a product for which someone will be willing to exchange cash. You have to create something. You have to take action and actually do something. Don't expect it to come just like that. I'll say some more about how you can begin to take action a bit later. I encourage you to get into the mindset that acknowledges that to be successful and to develop your ideas is going to take a lot of hard work. And that's ok. Hard work is good. It's the vehicle to get you where you want to go.

3. Learn to manage your money well

Starting today, if you haven't done so already, I recommend that you open a personal savings account. I say this because all the successful people I know or have met, have developed the habit of saving. One of my mentors once said to me, "If you don't know how to save money, the seeds of greatness are not in you".

The key to good money management is deciding where your money is going to go even before you receive it. We do this by keeping what's called a budget.

Let's say that you get £10 per week pocket money every Friday. The person with a poor money attitude will likely go out and start spending straight away without giving any real though to it. What you, as somebody who is going to be a successful entrepreneur will do is think and plan in advance about what you will do with your money. Remember, you want your money to grow. Below is an example of how your weekly budget might look if you are earning £10 per week.

My Budget

Income	
Pocket Money	£10

Expenditure	
Savings	£1
Church/Charity	£1
Business Idea	£1
Social, Friends, Music, Games, etc.	£7

This is based on just earning £10 per week. If you did this consistently for one year, at the end of year 1 you will have saved £52 in your personal savings and £52 for you to invest in your business. If, for any reason, you need to buy a gift for someone or should an emergency arise, you will have some spare cash available. From today, start using a budget and tell your money where it is going to go instead of wondering where it all went.

The*sure* **way** to attain the wealth you desire is to spend less than you earn and to save the difference. Not all of the rich are rich because they earn a lot of money; the rich are rich because they saved a lot of money. They understand the power of compound interest.

Consider two individuals, we'll call them John and Tom. Both John and Tom are the same age. When John was 25 he invested £15,000 at an interest rate of 5.5%. For simplicity, let's assume the interest rate was compounded annually. By the time John reaches 50, he will have £57,200.89 (£15,000 x [1.055^25]) in his bank account.

John's friend, Tom, did not start investing until he reached age 35. At that time, he invested £15,000 at the same interest rate of 5.5% compounded annually. By the time Tom reaches age 50, he will have £33,487.15 (£15,000 x [1.055^15]) in his bank account.

What happened? Both John and Tom are 50 years old, but John has £23,713.74 (£57,200.89–£33,487.15) more in her savings account than Tom, even though he invested the same amount of money! By giving his investment more time to grow, John earned a total of £42,200.89 in interest and Sam earned only £18,487.15.

This is why I encourage you to start saving and investing as soon as possible. In the short-term, it doesn't make a huge difference — but don't let that fool you. Short-term results are not as important as what will happen over the course of 20 or 30 years.

4. More money won't necessarily make you more happy

You CAN make money. In fact you can make lots of money if you so choose. I hope that when you do make a lot of money you will do lots of good things with it.

There have been lots of people who have been in the same position that you are in right now. Desiring to start a business, to be their own boss and be successful and wealthy, in the hope that they will have a happier life. Of course, money can make your life much happier. Realise though that there are a lot of rich and unhappy, suicidal and depressed people in the world. Many of them pursued money in the hope of finding happiness and never did. Happiness depends on a lot more than money. Some of the happiest people I have ever met have been living in some of the most remote villages in Africa. They have to walk miles to get water, or go to school and live in huts, yet they are often extremely happy people. I'll say it again: Happiness depends on a lot more than money.

If someone is currently unhappy in their life and the root of their unhappiness is a lack of money, then having more money can quite likely make them more happy. However, several reports have shown that when people have a really bad attitude towards money, and they get a sudden windfall of cash, like winning the lottery, it often doesn't end well. In fact there are stories all across the internet of millionaire lottery winners going broke in a matter of months, or a few years and their lives being left in tatters.

Don't expect money to be an end in itself. Don't depend on it for your happiness. It will change your life. It will allow you to change the world in a meaningful way, but don't count on it for your happiness. Find that within. I hope you get that. It's important to understand this as early as possible.

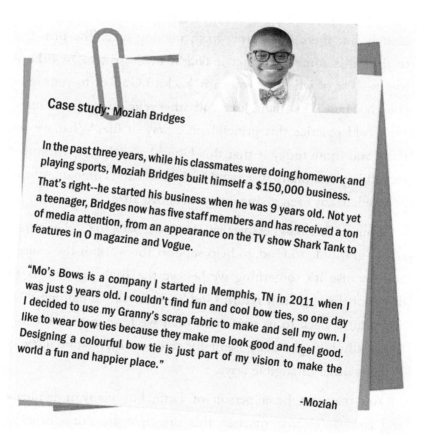

Case study: Moziah Bridges

In the past three years, while his classmates were doing homework and playing sports, Moziah Bridges built himself a $150,000 business. That's right--he started his business when he was 9 years old. Not yet a teenager, Bridges now has five staff members and has received a ton of media attention, from an appearance on the TV show Shark Tank to features in O magazine and Vogue.

"Mo's Bows is a company I started in Memphis, TN in 2011 when I was just 9 years old. I couldn't find fun and cool bow ties, so one day I decided to use my Granny's scrap fabric to make and sell my own. I like to wear bow ties because they make me look good and feel good. Designing a colourful bow tie is just part of my vision to make the world a fun and happier place."

-Moziah

"A good reputation is more valuable than money"–King Solomon

5. Be generous with your money but not foolish

To be generous is to be willing to give; whether you give to those in need, to good causes or charity. Practice being a giver and I can personally testify that you will see abundance flowing back into your life in various ways.

You will notice in the budget I outlined earlier that I recommended you gave 10% to your church or a charity. Obviously, not everyone reading this book is going to be connected to a church, but there is a point worth making here. The principle of tithing is something that is taught in the Bible. To tithe is to give 10% of whatever you earn 'back to God' or to your local church. Many Christians, Jews and other religious people around the world practice this principle as a way of life. What we see more and more today is that this biblical principle of tithing is something that many successful individuals and companies have adopted. Many even giving over and above 10%.

From a Christian perspective, we give it back to God as a sign of our gratitude to God, to help support the work of the church and because it's something we believe the Bible teaches us to do. We believe that in return God 'protects' the remaining 90% and returns back to us way more than we have given. Not just financially, but spiritually, mentally, emotionally, relationally and in many other intangible ways.

You may not be a person of faith, but many individuals and companies that practice this principle are not Christian companies, yet they understand and value the benefits and so do it anyway.

To be foolish with your money is to be wasteful. It is to spend what you don't have when the right thing to do is to delay the gratification and wait until you have the money enough to do what it is you need to do. We all like 'nice things' and there is nothing wrong with that. However, spending what we don't have on 'nice things', unnecessary luxuries and inessentials, whilst not saving and paying our bills is a recipe for disaster. That may sound a bit obvious to you but I guarantee if I asked 10 adults if they have experienced being in this trap, at least half would say yes.

STUDY MONEY

As part of your self education plan, I would like you to read up on money. There are some fantastic books available that will help you to get a deeper understanding of how money works. What I'm sharing with you about money and wealth creation in this book is merely an introduction and an overview. There are some fantastic books available on the subject of money that will help you to get a much deeper understanding on how money works. 'Wired for Wealth' by Brad Klontz and 'Rich Dad Poor Dad' by Robert Kiyosaki, are great examples to get you going. I have included a recommended reading section at the end of this book.

Who do you know who is successful? Maybe, if you're very fortunate, it's your mom or dad. Otherwise, it may be a relative or family friend or a member of your community or a business person in your city. If you think about it long and hard enough and take the limitations off your thinking, I'm sure you will begin to see that there are lots of hard working successful people all around you.

As a homework assignment, I want you to contact three of them and arrange a meeting or interview with them. Either in person or on the phone/Skype. There's no need to be nervous. This is something we call 'networking'. I'll say more about networking in the next chapter. They're probably going to be very willing to give you their time and their support. When you meet them I want you to take the time to discuss with them their answers to following questions:

1.   Why and what was your motivation for going into business?

2.   How did you get started?

3.   Please tell me the story surrounding your most rewarding achievement

4.   Please tell me the story surrounding the biggest challenge you've had to face

5.   What advice could you give to me about how to manage my money at my age?

Then note down what you learned from the answers given to each question.

1.

2.

3.

4.

5.

ACTION:

1. Money is neutral. It only magnifies who you are.

If you had great wealth think of all the positive things you would choose to do for:

-   yourself

-   your family

-   your community

-   to support a cause or address a disadvantage that's close to your heart.

2. Money follows service and hard work. In order to get paid and earn money, you need to provide a service or create a product for which someone will be willing to pay.

3. If you don't save money, the seeds of greatness are not in you.

Have you opened a savings account?

If you haven't – that's your first priority. Look on-line and find the best one for you.

If you have opened one decide exactly how much you will save – each week, each month, each year. Decide on a minimum amount. Decide what % of your income you will save.

4. The key to good money management is deciding where your money is going to go even before you receive it by keeping a budget.

What are the important headings in your budget?

What is essential?

What is something you could manage without if you needed to change or reduce your budget?

5. Don't expect money to be an end in itself. Don't depend on it for your happiness. Happiness depends on a lot more than money – it may just enhance your happiness in certain areas of life.

Find your happiness from within.

Decide what makes you really happy:

think of thoughts, feelings when you know you're happy

-   think of relationships about which you are happy

-   think of situations that promote happiness

What positive impact (if any) could money have on any of these?

6. Practice being a giver and you will see abundance flowing into your life in various ways. It's like depositing your savings – you deposit positively by giving to others, the positivity around you grows, with interest!

Decide on some ways that you can help those around you – your family, your friends, your community – that will have a positive impact and is sustainable.

CHAPTER 3

How to handle the pressure when it comes

"Everything negative—pressure, challenges – is all an opportunity for me to rise."

—Kobe Bryant

It's Sunday 8th February 2015 and its the final of the African Cup ofNations football tournament. In the final are Ghana and the Ivory Coast. The stakes are high. Ivory Coast have made it to the final twice in recent years, only to lose both games after a penalty shootout. There's a lot to play for and both teams are desperate to lift the trophy.

After 90 minutes its still 0-0 and the game is sent into extra time. After a further 30 minutes of extra time still no goals are scored and the match is sent to penalties. The dreaded penalties. The pressure is on. With all the remaining outfield players successful with their kicks, it was left to the respective goalkeepers to play out the final drama.

Up first, the Ghanaian keeper Razak Braimah. With the world watching his every move, he approached the ball, shuffled his feet, and...its saved. Subsequently, Boubacar Barry the Ivorian keeper stepped up to take the deciding penalty. He knew that if he scored he and his team would make history. That his life would change forever. He scored, and Ivory coast were victorious.

One highly pressured situation, two very different responses and of course two different outcomes. The fact is, when under pressure many people find that they are not able to produce their best performance. It is a very common experience, and failure — when the occasion matters most — is a very unpleasant experience.

Pressure is something we all have to face at some point in our lives. It might be the pressure of facing a forthcoming examination or test. It might be the pressure of having to deliver a presentation to a group of people, or the pressure that comes from your friends or peers. Pressure comes in various guises. In business you are also likely to face pressure. Whether its the pressure of deadlines. Meeting certain quality standards or paying staff, pressure can come from a number of sources. What's important is that we learn strategies that helpus to handle pressure effectively when it arrives.

When I was about 14 years old, around 5 of my friends and I had gotten up to no good and found ourselves in trouble with the police. We were given a stern telling off by the police but that wasn't enough for our parents. They wanted to know the details of exactly what had happened and who had done what. All of our parents very wisely teamed up together to set up a mock court room in my friend's front room. One by one we were called in to each give our version of events.

I met with each of my friends one by one beforehand and carefully briefed each of them, and we agreed what we would say. Our stories were perfectly put together. At least that's what I thought. Once all of the 'interviews' were concluded they called us all in together. My dad was the spokesperson for the parents. He said "We've listened to all of you and Errol we've proved that you are the culprit!" "What?!" I panicked. I didn't know what to say. Thinking that I had genuinely been caught I owned up. Only the truth was, they had no idea who it was. My dad was calling my bluff and I completely fell for it. Hook, line and sinker. I was so scared of my dad that I couldn't hide it. Again I was in big, big trouble.

I was in a position where I was in the wrong but felt that it was ok to cover the situation up, whether out of fear or just craftiness, this was the mindset and attitude with which I went through my teenage years. I wasn't trustworthy and I lived by the code that no-one else could be trusted either.

If you're going to be someone that is able to handle pressure effectively here are a few things I think you should do.

1. Becoming a truth-teller

Listen, you don't want to be like I was. If you think and behave like I did then you are not likely to succeed at all. I want you to start building the kind of character that will help you to handle any pressure that might come your way on your journey to success. The point of this chapter is to give you some practical advice that will help you to have enduring success. Not the kind that is a bit like a firework which goes up in the sky, makes a big bang and then disappears, but instead be someone that stays the course, avoids unnecessary controversy and maintains a healthy and lasting reputation.

My hope for you is that you will have 'good success'. The type of success that leaves a positive and lasting memory of who you were and what you did. Not the kind that ends in tragedy, moral failure, or as a scandalous story on the front page of a tabloid newspaper.

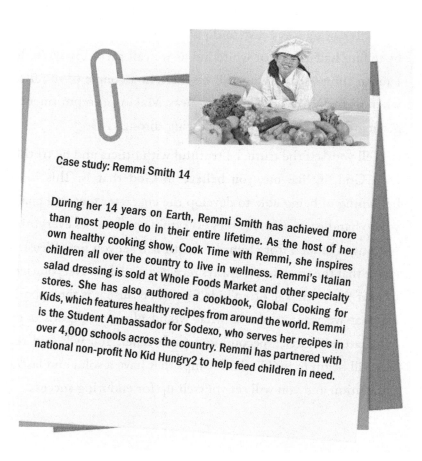

Case study: Remmi Smith 14

During her 14 years on Earth, Remmi Smith has achieved more than most people do in their entire lifetime. As the host of her own healthy cooking show, Cook Time with Remmi, she inspires children all over the country to live in wellness. Remmi's Italian salad dressing is sold at Whole Foods Market and other specialty stores. She has also authored a cookbook, Global Cooking for Kids, which features healthy recipes from around the world. Remmi is the Student Ambassador for Sodexo, who serves her recipes in over 4,000 schools across the country. Remmi has partnered with national non-profit No Kid Hungry2 to help feed children in need.

Essential to you having this kind of success is becoming a truth teller. A truth teller is someone that speaks the truth in all situations. The example I gave of not being a truth teller in the story I shared above, happened when I was a teenager. As a teenager those bad decisions had few consequences, apart from me being disciplined by my parents. However, the older you get in life, the more responsibility and recognition you receive the more important those decisions become.

I have made the decision to do my best to tell the truth at all times. It's not always easy to do when you have gotten by in life by telling half-truths or white lies as we call them. By white lies I mean things like saying "I'll be there in a couple of minutes", when really I'm 10 or 15 minutes away, Making a commitment to getting things done and not following through.

Tell yourself the truth, be truthful with others and be truthful with God, if, like me, you believe in God that is. This is the beginning of being able to develop the character that will enable you to handle pressure. He sees everything and knows everything, nothing is hidden from him. The truth will set you free. Please be aware that the truth is not always received well. Not everyone likes to hear the truth. We often hide from it because it is the opposite of what we want to do or what would please us. Truth is our true nature. Practice becoming a truth-teller. You will find that you will begin to build relationships that have a solid and lasting foundation and you will set yourself up for enduring success.

CHARACTER IS WHO YOU ARE WHEN NO ONE IS LOOKING

The person that you are on the inside will manifest on the outside. Privately, if you are a bit of a trickster, always looking for shortcuts or ways to turn things around for your favour at the expense of others it will be reflected in the outcomes achieved.

In time, the real person we are will always find its way to the surface. It's the same for us all. There's no way of covering it up. The person that we are behind the scenes, when no one else is around, is who we really are. If you, or I, are going to be the type of person who has long and enduring success, we have no choice but to take a good, hard look at our private lives.

This means examining the following

- The quality of the choices that we make about our lives.

- The way we manage and spend our money.

- The quality of the relationships that we choose to keep, especially those we spend most time with.

- The quality of character and attitude of the people that we spend most time with will give a good indication of where our life is heading.

When I speak about character to students in schools, I use the example of the train and the train track. Imagine the most amazing train in the world. It can travel at super-high speeds, it has a leather interior. Wide screen TVs, all your favourite food, a spa, a sauna, you name it. What an amazing train that would be! Now, the train represents your gifts or your skill set. The train track represents your character and integrity, as described above. We can have the best train in the worldwith all the nice things listed above, all the talents and gifts possible to man. But without that track, the train is going nowhere. Without character we are not going to be able to move forward and utilise those gifts and talents to their fullest extent. Character is the difference maker.

2. Surround yourself with people that will support you and help you to grow

There's a great verse in the Bible that says "Do not be misled, bad company corrupts good character". (1 Corinthians 15:33)

I've touched on it before but it's so important that I think it's worth mentioning again. You and I will be just like the people that we spend the most time with. Why? Because our view of life, our attitudes and behaviour are shaped by relationships. If we choose to spend time around people of bad character, we end up assimilating their ways, and as good as we might have thought ourselves to be, we find ourselves doing things we wish we hadn't.

We will never be bigger than the quality of the conversations that we have with the people around us. People that are excelling in life are those that have helpful and fruitful conversations. Naturally uplifting people. Likewise, those who feel stuck or resigned in life are likely to be those that spend their time moaning, complaining or being negative. You really have to take a look at the circle of people you associate with and do an assessment of the level of conversation you are having and ask whether these conversations are moving you closer to, or further from your purpose.

The mistake that we sometimes make is to believe that we can 'rescue' our friends who have negative mindsets. I have had to learn the hard way that you or I can't rescue anyone. You and I should be the kind of people that, when we hear the level or quality of conversation dropping or getting negative, we lift the conversation higher. You and I are carriers of hope, we inject and infuse possibility into everyone we meet. However, it's not your job to change someone.

3. Be flexible and open to change

Being flexible and open to change is important if you are going to be able to handle pressure when it comes. Some people are like an oak tree, strong and firm, refusing to bend, even under the fiercest wind or gale. The successful person will be more like a reed blowing in the wind. They shift and adjust in times of change. They're not afraid to do things differently and learn new things if needs must.

There are three key factors that will determine your ability to change when pressure comes. You change because

1. You have the desire to change.

2. You believe that change is possible.

3. You believe that change will be of benefit to you.

- **Having the desire to change**

Do you have a desire to change in some way? Your desire to change comes from having a sense of responsibility, ambition or calling in your life. This doesn't always come naturally. It can be divinely inspired, or it can be brought about by a unique set of circumstances, like the loss of a loved one or a bad accident. It can happen at any stage in life. The key thing is that, without this desire first being there, it is impossible to change. The more fortunate ones amongst us, were raised in environments in which we were challenged to grow and to realise our full potential. In such cases, the desire to improve or grow comes almost naturally. Not everyone has the same impulse and in some people the resistance to change is huge. People become content with the status quo and their standard of living, and their desire drains from them. For you, or anyone else to change the desire must first be there.

- **Believing that change is possible**

Do you really believe that you actually CAN change? Having the desire to change is one thing, believing that you can change is something else. You might see other people around you achieving success. Their success might even stir up some desire in you for a better quality of life or for different possibilities, but you still may not believe that change is possible for YOU. This is where confidence comes in. Believing in yourself even when the odds are not in your favour. Taking the risk of stepping outside of your comfort zone to try something different having no guarantee of the outcome. You can do it. Change is possible. Positive change is possible for you.

Case study: Maddie Bradshaw, Founder of m3 girl designs

Maddie Bradshaw is the President of m3 girl designs, a jewellery company, with annual revenues of around $1.6 million, selling over 60,000 necklaces per month in over 6,000 U.S. retail outlets, including Amazon.com and Nordstrom. Everything started when Maddie was 10 years-old and wanted to decorate her school locker, but couldn't find anything interesting and original. When her uncle, who had an old Coke machine, gave her 50 bottle caps, she decided to decorate them herself and put magnets on them. The now 16-year-old recalls: "When my friends saw the caps, they wanted me to make some for them."

Their enthusiasm made Maddie determined to try something new: design necklaces with a metal pendant to attract the bottle cap, which she called Snap Caps®. The Snap Caps aim to capture and celebrate every girl's unique personality, with themes ranging from initials, music stars and fairy tales. Bradshaw took 50 of the necklaces to a local toy store. In less than two hours, they sold out. The young entrepreneur remembers: "At that point, I knew I was onto something. [...] I think we were successful in the beginning because I was more focused on having fun and less worried about failing." Even though she only spent $300 of her own money, matched by her mother, to buy supplies, Maddie had already made her first million by the age of 13.

Maddie, alongside her younger sister, Margot, who is the company's vice-president, creates the jewellery designs. She also attends all the company's meetings and trade shows. The young entrepreneur has recently added a new line of necklaces, called Spark of Life, which targets an older group, teens. She revealed: "The great thing about our company is that it's growing with me. [...]As my tastes change, so will the products."

Bradsaw has also published a book, called You Can Start a Business, Too, after receiving numerous emails from young girls who also wanted to start a business. At the same time, she is striving to create a scholarship to help aspiring young entrepreneurs, as she confessed: "I love that I have an opportunity to reach out and help others. [...] Not everybody has the money like I did to pay for start-up costs."

Source: takingonthegiant.com

How to Build Your Belief

One way to build your belief is to clearly identify the obstacles or potential pitfalls that might prevent you from making your change, or from achieving your goal. When working with teenagers I ask them to complete the following exercise.

I first ask them to draw three fairly large circles on a piece of paper, one circle inside another like you can see in the diagram below. I then ask them to write in the inner circle exactly what their goal is. To write down exactly what it is that they want to achieve or change.

In the second circle I ask them to write down all of the potential pitfalls or dangers that might prevent them from achieving those desired goals. Here they will again make a comprehensive list of all the things that might hold them back in some way.

Lastly, they will write in the third circle all of things that they need to do in order to eliminate the dangers and pitfalls that they have written down in the second circle I ask them to be as detailed as possible and to make sure they come up with at least one thing they can do to eliminate each of the dangers mentioned in the 2nd circle.

The results are often very enlightening for the person completing the exercise. The exercise empowers them and gives them to ability to see exactly what needs to be done to achieve their goals and gives them the confidence to believe they can do it. They can see that if they focus on getting the things done that they have identified in the third circle, the desired result is very, very achievable.

Here is an example of a circle that was completed by Alisha. Her goal was to get A's and A* in her GCSE exams.

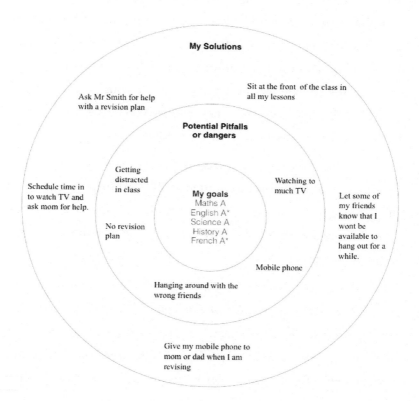

I really recommend that you conduct the same exercise for your idea or for a particular goal you have or change you want to make.

- **Believing that change can be of benefit**

So you have a desire for change and a belief that change is possible, but do you see a benefit in making the change?

You see, if someone doesn't believe that there is a positive benefit or favourable outcome if they make a change or you don't see that making the change is going to improve your life in some way, then you are very unlikely to even attempt it. You've got to be clear about the positive benefits of the change you desire to make, both for you and for those around you. Ask yourself whether the result of the change will bring you closer to your purpose or goal in life? Will achieving the outcome move you closer to alignment with or further away from your core values.

These are questions that need to be pondered as you attempt to bring about transformation in your life and turn your pressure or challenge into a place of opportunity. If any one of these three factors are not in place, then the change is going to be very unlikely to happen.

Consider the case of Rebecca. Rebecca was a talented singer. She had become very popular in her local community because of her singing ability. She would often perform at big events, community performances and, occasionally, she would be asked to perform as a support artist for recognised international acts that had flown in on tour.

What made the significant difference for Rebecca was her Youtube channel. Her videos had become so popular that she was getting 100's of thousands of views. This meant that in some parts the country she was very popular and even a household name amongst some communities.

I spoke with Rebecca when she had come to a point where she was feeling apathetic and hopeless about her prospects in the music business. Wanting to pack it all in if the next single release didn't bring her in a significant amount of cash. I was surprised at her attitude. I had heard some of her music and seen the response that she had gotten to some of her videos online. She was very highly respected.

In her mind, she had decided that although she had gotten some good feedback and built a big following, her goals were out of reach. She couldn't see how it would be possible to leverage what she had already done and turn her passion, music, into a profitable career.

I challenged her on her views. "Why do you think this career isn't worth pursuing?"

"Aww I just live in the wrong part of the country, for me to even stand a chance, I'm going to have to move out of this city and go to one of the big cities". "What makes you say that?" I asked. "I've seen it so many times, people just like myself, getting turned away because we don't come from the big city or other people from the big city being preferred to us."

"Have you ever seen anyone not from the city that has broken through?" I asked.

"Yeah of course. But they are few and far between. Plus I don't know any of the right people for me to get connected to." I listened as she poured out excuse after excuse as to why she would be unable to realise her full potential in this area of her life. It was fair to say that she had been on the receiving end of a great deal of rejection and opposition in recent times. A look at some of the friends that she hung around with and the way they spoke, gave the impression that birds of a feather had flocked together. They talked the same, behaved the same and were alike in attitude.

Never stay stuck! You're never more than one conversation or one question away from your breakthrough!

I began by first getting her to clarify exactly what her goal was. What it was EXACTLY that she wanted to achieve. "I want to sell 10,000 albums" she said. I wasn't convinced that we had still gotten down to the real goal but because of time I moved on in the process. I asked three or four questions one after the other, giving time in between each one to give her a chance to answer:

"What have you done so far to achieve that goal?"

"Who is there around you that can help you or work with you to accomplish that goal?"

"What else can be done or needs to be done to help you get there?"

"What difference will achieving that goal make to your life?"

As she began to answer these questions and I dug deeper into some of her answers her eyes began to light up. Her countenance changed. She was beginning to believe that the success she desired was possible.

She realised that although she hadn't acknowledged it, there was a long list of people both home and abroad that had supported or encouraged her over the years that would be willing to continue to support her now. She had more people, networks and resources on her side than she had realised.

She drew up a long list of these people, some she didn't have contacts for, but she vowed to Google them and track them down. As the lights came on in her head she became visibly more confident and she now had an action plan that supported her towards achieving her goal. We agreed to check back in a couple of weeks to see how she was getting on.

One of the big reasons people stay stuck or give up, is a lack of confidence in themselves and in their abilities to achieve the level of success they desire. In the next chapter we will look more closely at the whole topic of confidence.

ACTION:

1. Take control–create your own version of events.

How are you going to produce your best performance when the stakes are high with a lot of pressure?

We feel pressure in a number of ways. it's important to learn strategies that can help you to handle pressure effectively when it arrives.

In which situations, that are really important to you, do you feel most under pressure?

Decide what it would be like to rise to the challenge, make the most of that situation and perform well. What would it feel like? What would if look like? What would people around you say about your performance?

Now think of all the things you can do to create you're your positive version of events.

What practical things can you do to make it happen? Who can help you?

Make a plan to ensure you perform at your best.

Now mentally rehearse the situation going exactly as you want it to go. If doubts creep in, keep coming back to your positive version of events.

2. Practice becoming a truth teller.

Cut out the lies – even the little ones that you think don't matter. It will enable you build relationships that have a solid and lasting foundation and you will set yourself up for enduring success.

3. The attitudes of the people that we spend most of the time with will give a good indication of where our life is heading.

Beyond immediate family, and the teachers you're allocated at school you can decide the people you want in your life. Make that decision.

Create a map of the 10 people who have most influence in your life. Put yourself in the centre and group people round you – those with most influence nearest to you and those with least influence furthest away.

Now, for each person reflect on the following:

- What do they positively bring to your life?

- How are they helping you to develop and grow as a person?

- How can they help you make the changes you need to make?

- Can you really rely on this person in the things that are important to you?

- In what ways may they be a negative influence in your life?

- What can you do to minimise that negative influence?

Who do you want to be the 5 closest people to you to help you become the person you choose to become?

NB There are some people in our lives that we can't control – immediate family, teachers – but we can ensure we manage our relationship with them to make sure we make the most of how they contribute to our lives and minimise the negative bits.

'You're the average of the five people you spend the most time with'.
Jim Rohn

4. Be Willing to Change – when it's important to enable you to realise your goals

Three factors that will determine your ability to change:

Having the desire to change

Believing that change is possible

Believing that change will be of benefit to you.

Decide 3 things you want to change that will help you realise your goals.

Tell people who can help you.

Make a plan.

Go to work and make it happen.

Case Study: Jordan Casey, 13

Jordan Casey is a 13 year old Entrepreneur from Waterford, Ireland. He Founded TeachWare in early summer 2013 when he was just about to finish school for summer break. His saw that his Teachers were made to use outdated systems for student management, such as attendance, homework, exams and just general information. He saw that it could be so much easier and modern, and over the summer he began work on a project to do exactly that, modernise and simplify the way teachers go about their business.

CHAPTER 4

Building your confidence and self belief

"With confidence, you have won before you have started."
—Marcus Garvey

What if? What if the ambitious amongst us in our generation, whether they were straight-A students, or not, or whether they had the necessary and beneficial parental support, could still find a way to develop their mindsets and attitudes and make a great and positive contribution to the society in which we live?

I believe that this is absolutely possible for every ambitious young person out there. In fact, the times that we live in and the technology available to us, make it more and more possible. I'm convinced of this for a number of reasons. Firstly, in travelling to different countries around the world I have seen time and time again individuals that, in-spite of life's hardships and limitations, have been able to rise above, breakthrough and make a difference in their community, city or nation. Which demonstrates that, if you have the ambition to be able to live a life that matters and a life that leaves a lasting legacy and a strong enough 'WHY', YOU CAN DO IT!

I'm also convinced because throughout my favourite book, the Bible I see stories of individuals that overcame the odds. They came from lowly backgrounds, but by applying some of the principles I'm am sharing with you in this book, they turned their lives around. In addition, I'm convinced because, my own life and story is evidence that it is possible. Despite what others may have said or thought about me in the past, I have chosen to take responsibility for my own growth and development and not to leave it in the hands or my teachers, parents, or anyone else for that matter.

I've had the privilege of being able to speak to thousands of people each year, young and old, sharing my story and the lessons learned, inspiring individuals to make the most of their lives and overcome any limitations. I passionately believe that if it's possible for me, then of course you, and those around you, can do it too.

The thing is, the confidence you need to be successful as a young entrepreneur or business owner doesn't grow on trees. Our confidence develops over time as we step out and take action on the ideas that we have. If there was a formula for confidence, I think it would look something like this:

Action + Feedback + Reflection + Action = Confidence.

Notice, it doesn't necessarily matter whether the feedback is good or bad. The purpose of the feedback is to help you correct your course and do it better next time.

Larry Page the CEO of Google once said "You'd think that as we do more ambitious things, our failure rates would go up, but it doesn't really seem to. The reason, I believe, is even if you fail in doing something ambitious, you usually succeed in doing something important." I like to use the example of our first attempt at creating AI, which was started when Google had less than two hundred people back in 2000. We did not succeed in creating an AI, but we did come up with AdSense, where we target search ads against web pages, which has become a good chunk of our revenue. So we failed at making AI, but we got distracted by something useful. Pretty much 100 percent of these things have gone that way." (Source Bold Book, P Diamandes, 2015)

Thomas Edison was famous for being one of individuals responsible for inventing the light bulb. Over 10,000 of his experiments came to nothing. When asked by people why he had bothered persisting with his experiments after having failed so many times he said, "I've not failed, I've only found 10,000 ways how not to do. Thankfully, he and his team persisted and eventually achieved their goal.

Here are some things that you can do to build your confidence and the kind of resilience you will need to have for you to be successful as a young entrepreneur.

1. If someone else has already achieved it so can you

I described earlier that my own start in life was a challenging one. Please allow me to share my personal story with you in a bit more detail. I came from a difficult background. My parents divorced when I was 11 years old, my father was absent for most of my teenage years. I got involved in gangs and with drugs from the age of 13. I attended a grammar school having passed my 11 plus but my mind was always on the streets. I had very little motivation and didn't feel accepted anywhere other than on the streets. At the age of just 16, I found myself homeless due to my delinquent behaviour and criminal lifestyle. My behaviour was too much for my mom too put up with whilst trying to raise three children on her own. (I go into more detail about my story in my first book "From the Postcode to the Globe".)

Yet despite that, at age 34 I have my own business, delivering leadership programmes in schools around the UK. I am a co-founder of a company in Ghana that focuses on developing the next generation of leaders in Africa, a place close to my heart. I have already published one book, this is my second, and more are to follow. I've had the opportunity to travel and to speak to people around the world. I have met some truly amazing people who have made significant contributions to the world today.

My hope is that from reading this book you will see that the limitations that you have placed on yourself, or that people have placed on you, can in truth, be overcome. Perhaps by reading this book you will be inspired to dream a new dream, start a project or enterprise that will provide a good service to others or give you a sense of hope for yourself and for others around you.

2. Your past doesn't determine your future

I can appreciate that there are some circumstances, such as being in prison or being severely disabled that may present significant challenges. However, in this book you will read stories of people who have overcome unimaginable situations by having a certain kind of mindset. All around the world, men and women have overcome setbacks to achieve their goals and dreams. Here's my selection of inspirational individuals that have overcome many challenges in their past to achieve great success.

There are many such people willing to give of their expertise but it's up to you to go and seek them out, share your experience and seek out their advice. And then, more importantly, take action on their advice. Find a friend or someone that will hold you accountable for taking action.

You've gotta have faith

Why did it take me so long to get started in business? A lack of faith played a part. Courageous and faith-filled people decide early to choose the future they want by setting clear goals. They decide which parts of the past get to come along with them or not and they utilise their present to create the future they desire. It takes real courage to do that. "Courageous people play to win, fearful people play not to lose"–*Dan Sullivan*.

To not have faith is to allow ourselves to be ruled by that feeling of "what will everyone else think?" "What will they say about me?" "Will they still like me?" I remember the first event that I ever organised. I had very little experience of running events or managing people. I just had an idea and a desire to make a difference in the lives of young people. Something sparked inside of me. I recognised that I had to do something to make a difference. I could either be part of the problem or part of the solution.

We all need someone or something to light that spark for us. That spark is in all of us. We were all born with a unique ability to do something significant, to make a lasting difference. That's my core belief. This is not theory. This has been my experience.

This book is written for those with ambition, those that deep down have a knowing that they are created for a purpose and they want to make it happen. Those that perhaps haven't had the best start, but want to make a positive difference in the world. Those that desire to leave a legacy for themselves and those that come after them and are willing to pay the price to do that. Abundance, opportunity and possibilities are everywhere and they are endless. It's time for you to soar.

We have all heard the statement, "It's not what you know, it's who you know". What the statement implies is that having knowledge and information and wisdom about a particular topic, subject or situation, is not enough to get you to where you want to go. In order to get to your desired destination, you are going to need the help and assistance of other people. The quality of these relationships will have a definite impact on how far and how fast you will get to your goal.

There are no limits.. Allow your mind to dream of the possibilities for you to create, build and contribute all around the world. Having a global mindset, whilst maintaining an awareness of your local context, will make it easier to see the opportunities that are right before your face.

3. You build your belief by taking action in the direction of your goals

Its time for you to DO SOMETHING. You have to begin somewhere. You are here for a significant reason. I don't believe you were created by chance. There will never be a better time in all of human existence than this for you to step out and try an idea. To create something and make something happen. What are you waiting for?

Avoid the traps of procrastination (putting things off) and perfectionism (trying to make everything perfect before you take action) that we so easily fall into. We tell ourselves that we have got to get everything 100% right before we proceed. We have to have all the details in place. That perfectionism leads to procrastination. We delay and delay, until nothing gets done.

It hasn't got to be perfect! There are a few careers in which you have got to be 100% accurate. If you're a brain surgeon or a pilot perhaps, then there is very little room for error. In the case of your idea if you are 80% there, then you need to start moving. Put something out there. Get the ball rolling. It's time to be brave now and step out. You can't steer a parked car. Get moving and make adjustments as you go. You can do it.

Consider the case of Victoria. Victoria was a great communicator and professional speaker. She had been through many challenges in her upbringing and her life had taken many turns and twists. Whenever she shared her story with friends or in public, audiences would be enthralled. Colleagues and friends urged Victoria to put her stories on paper and to share them with the world. She had enough stories and life experiences to write several books.

Victoria's response was, "I do want to write a book, but I need a bit more experience". Or she would say "I don't think I'm quite ready yet". She would find different reasons as to why she wasn't ready to put pen to paper, when in actual fact, she had volumes of information in her heart and head to change the world.

Can you relate to Victoria's story? I'm sure there is a business idea you need to start on, a song or book you need to write. It's time to step out on that idea, quit making excuses and break out!

In fact take the advice of a young lady I met recently in Ghana and DO EVERYTHING! Primrose is a young leader and entrepreneur from Ghana. She said, "I decided that I was going to take every opportunity that came my way. Whether it was volunteering or otherwise, even if I didn't want to do it, I did it for the experience and the opportunity to meet new people."

I also remember the words of another young man who said, "I'm coming for your spot, Errol! I'm going to go right past you and leave you trailing in my dust!" Those were the enthusiastic words of a budding entrepreneur that had joined a team in one of my businesses. He was passionate and hungry for success and

I welcomed his ambition and bravado. My response to him was "I see better than I hear." I knew that success didn't come easy to anyone. If becoming successful was easy everyone would be successful. I understood that making it to the top was going to be a marathon and not a sprint.

In his zeal, my young friend behaved as though success was going to come overnight. The reality is that we all get the level of success that we are prepared to work for. We have to be willing to take the action necessary for us to get to our goal. I wrote this book for dreamers, people with ambition that have come to a point in their journey where they feel confined, hemmed in, unsure about how to bring their goals to fruition.

I want you to clearly see how it's possible to bring about positive change in any area of your life. Providing you're willing to take action. Action that might feel risky or uncomfortable, you will see and understand that positive change is possible for you in your life.

It all starts with you taking action. Reaching out to people. Who is there around you in your community that you see as a positive role model that could be a mentor to you? Maybe they are closer than you think; a family friend, a neighbour. Maybe there is a book that has been written by someone that has achieved what you aspire to and through that book you can be mentored by that author from afar.

I know that the thought of reaching out to a mentor or a stranger can be quite daunting. However, I have found that successful people are actually very generous with their time and encouragement. They often appreciate that someone would taketime to reach out to them and ask their advice.

In my early twenties I met a man named Karl George. At the time, Karl was running an accountancy firm in the City, one that he had built from the bottom-up and was known as a highly successful practice. He had a reputation as being among a group of young high-flying leaders in the City.

He was also, at the time, involved in an organisation called 100 Blackmen,an international organisation set up to empower and nurture the potential within young black men. It was through this network I first metKarl. I quickly realised hewas the most successful man I had ever come into contact with and that there was a great deal that I could learn from him.

Thankfully, Karl had a passion to provide guidance and advice for young people like myself and an informal mentorship relationship began to develop. More than a decade later, this relationship continues and, over the years, has slowly grown into a mutually beneficial friendship. And in the same way that Karl gave his time to support me and encourage me towards my goals, I now give of my time to help others. That's how the cycle goes. It would be great if you were inspired to follow this same example of passing on what you know to others.

I highlight this because in order for you to achieve your goal and dream you are going to need the support of mentors who have already walked the walk and have achieved that which you desire to achieve. They have navigated the challenges, the twists and turns you are likely to face and can help you to avoid many of the mistakes that they made.

My relationship with Karl and with other men and women like Karl who have come in my life to mentor me has resulted in personal andbusiness growth and an increase in my confidence.

You've got to decide today to get out of that comfort zone and choose CONFIDENCE over COMFORT. What do I mean by that? We find confidence when we step outside of our comfort zone and do those things that we never thought possible. We don't get confident by sitting down and talking about what could be possible. We grow in confidence by taking action. It doesn't necessarily have to be something big that we do, it could be something small but we have to do something!

This is why it's so important for us to have goals for our lives. Big or small goals. although the bigger and more challenging the goals the more energy and passion they can create. Goals take us outside of our comfort zone and outside the familiar and give some challenge to our lives, without which we cannot grow. You're probably reading this book because you are up for a new challenge and are beginning to realise that, "if I don't do something with my life now, I'm going to get the same old results in my life". Embrace that sense of nervousness or excitement about taking on a new challenge, trying something new is all a part of the process. Don't wait for everything to be perfect before you act, step out and make the calls.

It's easy to get trapped in the security and comfort trap. Stuck in the rhythm of the nine to five routine, or relying on handouts or donations from others. This kind of attitude can actually cause us to lose motivation and, over time, rob us of our confidence and our willingness to take risks. This can happen even when we begin to achieve a measure of success. Complacency can set in when we get comfortable with the increased measure of security and success that our achievements have given us. We have to tell ourselves that these periods of comfort are only a temporary stage, giving us time to establish bigger goals. By continuously striving for bigger goals and achievement our confidence will always be greater than our comfort.

I hope you're hearing this message loud and clear. Nothing changes until you do something. So much for wishing on a star! You have got the potential and ability to do great things in your life and business. NO MORE PROCRASTINATION. Nothing changes until you DO SOMETHING. Decide today to make those three phone calls and get that idea moving forward. Also decide to find a mentor who you can connect with for advice and support on your journey.

Remember

ACTION:

1. Allow your mind to dream of possibilities for you to create, build and contribute all around the world.

Successful people take time to get clear on their 'WHY".

Reflect on your goals every day (See Action from Chapter 1)

2. Confidence develops overtime as we step out and take action.

Nothing changes until you do something.

Look at the action plan you've created for your goals and make sure you've done something every day:

Finish that plan

- Find out that piece of information
- Do that research
- Ask that question
- Make that call
- Finish that leaflet
- Watch that motivational video clip
- Avoid the traps of procrastination and perfectionism that we so easily fall into. Trying to make everything perfect before you take action.

We all get the level of success that we are prepared to work for. We have to be willing to take the action necessary for us to get to our goal.

3. Believe in Yourself

One of the big reasons people stay stuck or give up is a lack of confidence in

themselves and their abilities to achieve the level of success they desire. You are the only person who can build your belief.

Find a photo of yourself that you like – put it in the middle of a page and around it put all the positive qualities you have and the things you're good at. Put it somewhere where you can see before you go to sleep and when you wake. Use it every day to

Remind yourself every day of:

- the things you're good at;
- the things you're working to improve – to be the best version of you.

4. "Courageous people play to win, fearful people play not to lose" Dan Sullivan

What can you do to step outside your comfort zone and be brave? If you tackle one thing that is challenging for you it will expand the whole of your comfort zone. e.g..

a. Make an appointment to talk to an influential person who can help you and prepare a 2-minute pitch of what you're aiming to achieve and how you think they can help. Prepare. Practice with those who can help you. Do it and use the experience to improve your presentation.

b. Do something that you find physically challenging (without endangering yourself)

c. play a sport you've never played before
   - enter yourself for a race (could be a short fun race

or something more challenging) and then start to practice – running, cycling etc.

– visit a gym with a friend who you know works out all the time and ask for their help (people always love to help in an area they're confident in)

– do a bungee jump etc.

BE BRAVE – YOU'LL BE AMAZED AT THE RESULTS

CHAPTER 5

Become a confident communicator

"Communication–the human connection–is the key to personal and career success."

—Paul J. Meyer

"**O**kay Errol, 5 minutes to go. You're up next."

"I'm not going out there. No way!"

"What do you mean? It's your show, just go out and let the audience say well done, you deserve it."

"No, I can't do it!"

That was my reaction when I was first asked to go out and speak to an audience of a few hundred people. I went into a state of panic and anxiety. Even though it was at an event that I had coordinated and organised, I was quite happy to stay behind the scenes, pulling the strings and encouraging the performers. Perhaps because the artists had the confidence to get out on the stage that I didn't have, but wished I did.

Eventually they got me out there to receive a bunch of flowers and a round of applause from the audience but I had honestly never been so scared. I remember my friends in the audience telling me how nervous and scared I looked and they were right!

I knew that even though I was really scared to stand in front of a crowd I couldn't remain that way. If I was going to achieve my goals and dreams in life, I would no doubt have to become a master communicator, able to speak to an audience of any size and be able to deliver a confident speech or presentation.

How I was going to get from being a wallflower to an accomplished speaker, I had no idea. The thought of being on stage and exposed, frightened me. I had the utmost respect for the others in my team, who were able to go on stage and make everyone laugh, but I just could not see myself doing it.

Maybe you're in a similar position right now yourself and you're thinking to yourself that public speaking is something that you're terrible at. Hopefully my experience as I've detailed above highlights to you that all successful speakers start somewhere. All those people that you admire and think are great performers on stage were once novices andprobably fearful just like you . If I can do it, so can you.

A recent survey conducted by *Distinction* discovered that, of the executives and entrepreneurs surveyed, more than **86 percent** said being able to present effectively has a significant impact on their **income** and **success**.

In this chapter I want to give you some practical tips as to how you can begin to develop your public speaking and communication skills; in doing so, building your confidence and preparing you to move closer towards achieving your goals.

i. Remember that every successful speaker had to start somewhere:

Back in December 2005, I was asked to give my first sermon at our church. It was the Christmas Day message. Christmas Day was one of the most well-attended days in the church calendar. Even the most irreligious individuals would come out to celebrate at the Christmas Day service out of tradition. When I was given the opportunity to speak I considered it a great privilege and accepted it gladly.

As the day drew nearer the thought of delivering a sermon in front an audience of hundreds of people became more and more daunting. In our church there were a number of great orators, male and female, young and old. It seemed that they were all able to make the audience laugh, whilst delivering a powerful and challenging message. Something I couldn't see myself doing, yet here I was stepping into the shoes of these people. "I can't make people laugh," I thought. "How can I step into their shoes?"

I decided that I was going to spend time in fasting and prayer and hope that God would give me the direction and wisdom I needed. I read my Bible and prayed, read my Bible and prayed. My confidence in God to deliver the sermon was increasing but then I panicked. I wasn't confident in what I had to say. I became so concerned about giving the congregation something tangible and helpful to take away that I resorted to going online and

97

looking for recordings of audio Christmas messages. I listened to loads of them and made copious notes. I then combined my notes together and wrote out a sermon.

It made sense to me at the time. The message resonated with my spirit but honestly it was not my own. It was a miss-mash concoction of my thoughts and lots of other peoples'. I remember standing on the pulpit that Christmas Day and shaking like a leaf. Reading my sermon line for line, hardly lifting my head to take a breath; I read through it as quick as I could and got to the end of the message in no time at all. The Lord was surely with me because the response to the message was unbelievable. Numerous people came forward that day to make a decision to dedicate or rededicate their lives to Christ. I was in a state of shock that my presentation had got such a response.

I look back on that day now with fond memories and I smile because I know how scared I was and what it took me to get up on that stage and hold my own. And now, of course, years later and with much more experience, I can quite easily deliver a talk or sermon without having any notes. Most weeks I will speak to audiences of at least 100 people 2-3 times a week. Rather than being afraid to get up and speak, I now find great pleasure in getting up and sharing my stories or experiences or sermons with audiences.

The message here is that 'we all have to start somewhere'. I just had to go through some rough patches, that's all. The more you speak the better you will get. If you are serious about developing your speaking skills, my recommendation is that you join a speaking club, like the Professional Speaking Association where you will get opportunities to speak in front of an audience and receive constructive feedback and meet other like-minded individuals. Keep trying, never give up, in time you will grow in confidence and technical ability. If you speak more, you will speak better.

Case Study: Katelyn Lohr

Katelyn Lohr is not your typical teenager. At age 13, she launched her own company, Freetoes Brand, Inc., to sell her invention: socks without toes, which are now sold across North America in stores like Toys R Us, Hallmark and Learning Express.

What really makes Katelyn special is her passion for giving back. She has donated hundreds of pairs of her socks to Project Aftershock, supporting the recovery in Haiti.

ii. Take and make as many opportunities to speak as you can

When I approached the local secondary school to ask if I could deliver some motivational assemblies for the students and they gave me a chance, my speaking ability really roseto a new level. Up until that point, I'd spoken a lot within a church context but speaking in a non-church environment was quite foreign to me. School teachers seemed not to be the most confident communicators, standing in front of hundreds of students and they were very happy for me to come in and speak. I grabbed the opportunity with both hands. It proved to be a great outlet for my passion to inspire young people.

They were very grateful for me coming in to speak and requested that I come back in again, and again, and again! I was loving it. I was able to try out new material and experiment with different delivery styles. It was amazing.

Out of a conversation with the headteacher came the opportunity for me to deliver a leadership development programme for a small group of year 8 students that would last 6 weeks. I designed the course and delivered the six week course for free. The following year, they approached me again for the same programme, only this time they paid me to deliver it. They were also happy to refer me to other schools. A close friend of mine was a senior teacher in another school and, hearing of my success, invited me to present to a network of teachers. They all loved the programme too. I went from working in one school to over 30 different schools in a very short space of time. This all started from offering my services free of charge or doing what we call in the Professional Speaking Association – 'Giving a showcase'.

To say my confidence increased is an understatement. My confidence shot through the roof. I was able to speak to hundreds of students and keep them engaged throughout and get a spontaneous round of applause at the end of my talks. It was a great feeling. It made me want to become better and better and to share my story with even more young people. I had no idea what it was worth in monetary terms at the time. I found out later that speakers get paid hundreds, even thousands, of pounds to deliver these kinds of motivational talks. If you were a celebrity or household name you would get paid tens of thousands of pounds

That's how it begun for me and you can do exactly the same. Contact your local school, a nursing home, or a scout group. Practice in front of your friends and family. Look for opportunities to share your story and your message. Listen to the feedback and refine your message and your communication style and come back again. For you to grow as a speaker, you really have to understand that you don't get better by thinking or dreaming about being a speaker, you get better by getting out there and speaking. Start today by looking for opportunities to get out there and speak.

iii.   Learn from the best

As a youngster growing up one of my heroes was the Liverpool football player John Barnes. He was an absolute legend. I remember seeing him on TV and thinking, "wow, I want to be like him." He inspired me to become a Liverpool fan. Whenever

I played football with my friends, I would imagine myself being John Barnes. In my head I was him! I would do the tricks like he did and trying to impersonate him gave me a sense of confidence and increased ability. Can you relate to doing the same with some of your childhood heroes?

I had a similar experience after taking on my first ministerial position at a local church in Birmingham in 2007. I was sent away for a year to do some leadership training up in Manchester. The training consisted of lectures and practical hands-on ministry training. I look back over that year with fond memories. We had a number of different speakers from around the world come in and speak to us on a variety of leadership and ministry related subjects. These men and women were amazingly gifted communicators.

There was one particular communicator that we all looked forward to the most. His name was Glyn and he was the head of the leadership academy. Whenever he spoke, unlike some of the other speakers, I was completely engaged throughout. When he spoke everyone leaned forward in their chairs. Their ears pricked up and they were excited. He had this amazing ability to fully engage everyone in the room, to inspire you to believe that you were more than you realised. He had an energy, enthusiasm and stage presence that would inspire audiences of thousands of young people to action.

I remember saying to myself, "I want that". I want to be able to have that kind of impact and influence on the people I speak to. Glyn showed me that it was possible. I had the chance to sit down with Glyn on a couple of occasions and to find out how he crafted his talks. He showed me how he prepared and how he structured his talks. This was a great insight for me.

Then whenever I had the opportunity to speak, I would practice delivering my talks with the same level of energy and enthusiasm as he did. I would use the little techniques he had showed me to engage people. The more I experimented with things I'd seen Glyn and others like him do, the more I began to understand what would work for me and what would not. I observed the response of the audiences and took the feedback on board and I began to develop my own style of communicating.

I know some people might say it's wrong to imitate others, well I disagree. My advice to you is to learn from the best. Look at the speakers that you admire, whether they be in your local church, on TV or in theatre. Look at what they do and learn from them. Apply their techniques into your repertoire. It's perfectly okay to experiment with different things. Over a period of time, you will begin to work out what comes naturally for you and what gets the desired results.. Learn from the best.

iv. Get clear on what your core message is

Whenever you have to speak to a group of people, speak with passion. When I was studying and preparing for my role in Church leadership, one of my colleagues affectionately declared me the "hope man". "Interesting" I thought. He said "I can see that wherever you go in the future, they're going to be calling you the hope man. You're going to be going around sharing your testimony and your story with people and just giving them hope".

TEENPRENEUR: HOW TO BUILD A BUSINESS IN YOUR TEENS

These words stuck with me and I have actually watched those words manifest right before my eyes. Everywhere I go, people tell me how much they are inspired and encouraged by my story and by hearing me speak. How much they feel like they have they have more HOPE for the future and for what's possible for them. I'm confident that it's possible for anyone to have this same result when your core message is clear. Whether you're black or white, young or old, fat or thin, tall or short it's possible for you too.

It's not something that I try to do or have to think about doing. Whenever I get the chance to speak to a crowd, there is just something that comes out of me that wants to speak of hope and possibility. I have an inborn desire to see everyone be the best that they can be, in spite of where they are. If you cut me open, you would find on the inside these values of hope, faith, connectedness and possibility; things that deeply matter to me. And when I speak from that place, I can't help but be passionate. I can't help but speak with enthusiasm and energy because that's who I am. It's what I live for.

When I share my personal story of coming from a life of gangs and drugs and being homeless at 16 to becoming a minister, entrepreneur and coach, and I share from this place, it amplifies my message. Even some of the most challenging audiences in prisons and in some of the tough schools are listening intently.

No one wants a wet fish standing in front of them, boring them to death, sending them to sleep. We all want to hear someone that has something good to say, who says it with passion and confidence.

So what's your core message? If you had just one minute to talk to your ideal audience about the things that mattered to you the most, what would you say? What's the message or topic that when you think about sharing it, makes you say YES!! Find that thing and then speak FROM that place. You won't fail to engage with your audience. You won't get stuck for words. It will flow naturally from your heart and you will leave that stage feeling, like, YES!!

Case study: Madison Robinson 15, US

Founder of Fish Flops

Age: 15

At the age of 15, most girls are just learning about fashion. But Madison Robinson is already on track to becoming a millionaire thanks to an ingenious design for light-up flip-flops for kids. The teenager, from Galveston Island, Texas, came up with the idea for Fish Flops at the age of just eight. With the help of her father, Dan, and some 'friends and family financing' she was able to turn her drawings into product samples and sell the idea to retailers at trade fairs. Over 60,000 Fish Flops have been sold, which The Daily Mail estimates as equaling "retail sales of at least 1.2 million."

v. Remember it's not about you

It's been said on many occasions that the number one fear that people have is getting up on stage and speaking to a room full of people. I'm sure we can all relate to feeling that fear at some point. In fact, I can very acutely remember the fear that gripped me when I was asked to speak to an audience in my younger years. If I'm honest, I still get nervous before I get on stage now.

I realise that speaking is one of my gifts. It's a tool that I use to help me fulfil my calling and purpose in life. So it's impossible for me to allow fear to hold me back.

You might be feeling the same but are unsure about exactly how to overcome this fear. The first way to address the fear is to prepare well. What I would do is take the time to get my material put together well. Making sure I am confident in what I am going to say and how I am going to say it. Doing my research to ensure that I am confident in the quality of my content. After that, I may spend time rehearsing my talk, sometimes alone or in the presence of friends or family. This helps me to build my confidence.

I do my best to get to the venue well in advance of the time I am due to be on stage. If possible, I head to the stage area and have a walk around , getting a feel for the space that I will be using. I will get a feel for the venue and how the room is laid out, and begin to visualise giving my talk and how it will all go. This helps to relax me and prepare me mentally. You don't always get this opportunity, of course.

I'll then go around and speak to as many of the delegates or members of the audience as I possibly can. I'll get to know them, see what kind of people they are and what expectations they have. Getting a feel of the audience helps me to ensure that my message or talk has the right tone.. After speaking to a few people, I may even change my talk slightly to suit the audience.

Which brings me to my last point about fear. The number one thing I do to overcome it is to remember it's not about me, it's about my audience and I'm there to serve them. I'm there to give them something that will be useful for them to take away and improve their lives. I take the spotlight off myself and I put it on them. In doing so, I find that a great sense of gratitude for the opportunity and love for the audience is able to flow and dissipates any fear. I then just want to get out on stage and give them the very best of me.

vi. Give a clear introduction

Whenever someone is introduced to an audience there are a couple of things that immediately go through the mind of the audience members. They immediately begin to ask themselves "Who is this person?" and "Why is he/she the person speaking to us about this particular subject?" Your ability to answer this question clearly and as early as possible can make or break your presentation.

A great introduction will answer those two questions, whilst leaving the audience with a sense of positive expectation. Depending on the nature of the event I'm being asked to speak at, I will write my introduction and send it to the person that will be introducing me in advance of the event. I then have more confidence that I will get a good introduction. Although the person could still read what I have written in an unhelpful way.this is still better than turning up and the person making a complete mess of my introduction and setting me off on the wrong foot.

Here's and example of an introduction that I used for an event I spoke at recently that was read out by the host.

"At 16 Errol was a fully-fledged gang member and an everyday drug user, destined to end up either dead or in prison and already written off by society. He could have become just another everyday statistic. Now, as an author and co-founder of Emerge Leadership, an organisation that seeks to change young lives across Europe and Africa, he has become an inspiring icon to many, and a great success. Today, we will hear Errol's story and how Errol has managed to use the power in that story to help grow a successful speaking business. Please welcome Errol Lawson."

This introduction went very well and paved the way for what was a very well received talk. There are, of course, times when you don't have the pleasure of being introduced and you are forced to go on to stage without even your name being mentioned. This is not an ideal scenario at all but one that you have to be able to quickly adjust to. Remember your audience are asking "Who is this person and why are they coming to speak to us about this?"

If this happens I'll begin straight away by saying "Hi, my name is Errol Lawson, I'm a Leadership coach, an author and a Minister and the Director of a company called Emerge Leadership." (Tell them who I am) "And what we do is travel to schools around the UK and in Africa speaking to young people and teachers, helping them to develop their leadership skills, build their confidence and realise their aspirations. Today, I'm here to speak to you about x" (Tell them what I do). Then I will share my personal story of being involved in gangs and drugs and being homeless to turning my life around and becoming a successful author and entrepreneur. (This is my credibility piece. Tell them WHY I am the person to be standing in front of them to be talking about this particular subject)

Remember your introduction is always key, it can be the making of your presentation.

ACTION:

1. Every great communicator starts somewhere.

To develop your communication skills, take and make as many opportunities as possible to share and present your ideas and get feedback:

- speaking to people informally – seeing their reaction, listening to their questions and using that to get your message clearer and address questions before they are asked;
- making formal presentations;
- sharing your ideas via social media in posts, tweets, blogs;
- creating your profile – look at the LinkedIn profiles of people in similar fields and get ideas about how to create a profile with impact;
- gaining clarity in your written communication – one page summaries of your ideas with sub-headings and bullet points to make it easier for the reader to digest.

2. Being nervous and fearful is the norm

Nervousness is part of doing things that are important to you and doing things that are risky where you are putting your ideas, credibility and reputation in front of people.

The best way to overcome fear and deliver your message with confidence is to prepare well:

- structure ideas and information in an order that's logical for the audience

- mix things that speak to the heart and the head – stories with stats
- mentally rehearse – go over in your mind performing as you want to perform – with everything as you want it. If you make a mistake – rewind and make it how you want it.
- physically rehearse – by yourself and with others who are going to give you constructive feedback.

3. Remember that it's not about you.

It's about how your audience will benefit and what they will take away.

What's in it for them? How will they benefit? What problem will it solve?

How will it improve things?

How is your message different / interesting?

4. Structure – Structure – Structure – Said with Passion

Give a clear introduction. Your Introduction can be the making of your presentation.

Grab the audience's attention.

Very briefly give them your structure – what you're going to share with them.

Make key points with evidence – again trying to combine head and heart with examples – quantity and quality.

What are you asking for from the audience? Their support in some way? If so, in what way? Be clear about your ask – even if it's only feedback.

Sum up recapping on key points and ending with a memorable sentence, story, fact, quote.

Your audience will only engage if they believe that you believe what you're saying. Communicate with belief and passion.

SECTION 2

CREATING THE BUSINESS AND SHARING IT WITH THE WORLD

CHAPTER 6

What's the big idea?

"No matter what people tell you, words and ideas can change the world."

—Robin Williams

If you have an idea at this stage already, that's fantastic. You might want to skip right on to the next chapter. In this chapter I am going to help you to discover and develop your ideas. What if you want to go into business but you don't have a solid idea yet? Where should you go? How do you get started? Well, of course, you need a good idea to work on. The great thing is that ideas are not that hard to come by; they're absolutely everywhere. The trick is being able to develop our minds and ask the right questions that will enable us to see them.

One young man came to me and said Errol, I want to go into business at some point. "Why do you want to do that?" I asked. His response was that he wanted to be his own boss. He didn't want to have to work in an office all day and have someone else telling him what to do. He didn't want to limit what he was able to earn by a salary that someone else set for him. And, he wanted to work the hours that he chose and not the regular nine-to-five with just 2-3 weeks holiday each year.

"Ok, so whats your big idea?" I asked. "How are you going to get there?" At that point he became a little stuck. He'd seen his dad doing quite well running the family business, but he didn't see himself doing exactly the same line of work. He was only 15 and his aspirations were big. He shared two or three of his ideas with me. All ideas that he had started on but hadn't really put any real commitment into. He hadn't completely followed through.

DECIDE TO WIN

I spoke in section A of this book about commitment. Commitment is really important in the process of creating and developing ideas. The best ideas often come to us at times in our lives when our backs are against the wall and we have hit rock bottom. When we are forced to act or respond to the challenge at hand.

When I started my first business at 19, I literally had nowhere else to go. I was a college dropout. Living in a friends house, going nowhere in life. My initial idea was everything I had. I threw all of my energies and efforts into making it happen. At the time of writing this book, Im soon to be married. My fiancé is an amazing woman. Nothing is more motivating for me at this point in my life than the fact that I want make sure that I am able to provide for her and take care of her needs.I'm determined to give it everything I've got.

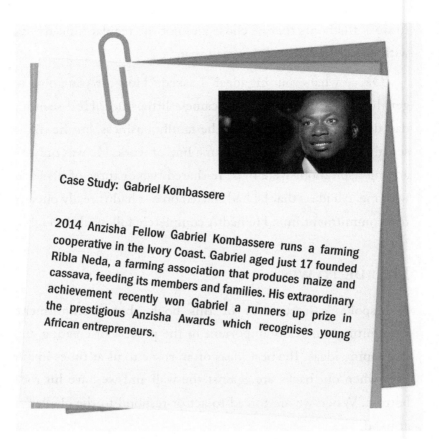

Case Study: Gabriel Kombassere

2014 Anzisha Fellow Gabriel Kombassere runs a farming cooperative in the Ivory Coast. Gabriel aged just 17 founded Ribla Neda, a farming association that produces maize and cassava, feeding its members and families. His extraordinary achievement recently won Gabriel a runners up prize in the prestigious Anzisha Awards which recognises young African entrepreneurs.

When we are in this state of mind, not only are we extremely motivated, but we come up with ideas all of the time. It's something called Human Ingenuity. It's the way we are wired as humans. When we find ourselves in a situation where the only was is up, we somehow find a way.

How badly do you want to get into business and achieve the quality of life you desire? Are you still in two minds about it? Are you saying that you might start a business, or are you thinking about starting a business someday? I encourage you to decide now exactly what you want to do. Once you make that all or nothing decision, your best ideas will start flowing.

MAKING STONE SOUP

Many years ago, three soldiers, hungry and weary of battle, came upon a small village. The villagers, suffering a meagre harvest and the many years of war, quickly hid what little they had to eat and met the three at the village square, wringing their hands and bemoaning the lack of anything to eat.

The soldiers spoke quietly among themselves and the first soldier then turned to the village elders. "Your tired fields have left you nothing to share, so we will share what little we have: the secret of how to make soup from stones."

Naturally the villagers were intrigued and soon a fire was put to the town's greatest kettle as the soldiers dropped in three smooth stones. "Now this will be a fine soup", said the second soldier; "but a pinch of salt and some parsley would make it wonderful!" Up jumped a villager, crying "What luck! I've just remembered where some's been left!" And off she ran, returning with an apronfull of parsley and a turnip. As the kettle boiled on, the memory of the village improved: soon barley, carrots, beef and cream had found their way into the great pot, and a cask of wine was rolled into the square as all sat down to feast.

They ate and danced and sang well into the night, refreshed by the feast and their new-found friends. In the morning the three soldiers awoke to find the entire village standing before them. At their feet lay a satchel of the village's best breads and cheese. "You have given us the greatest of gifts: the secret of how to make soup from stones", said an elder, "and we shall never forget." The third soldier turned to the crowd, and said: "There is no secret, but this is certain: it is only by sharing that we may make a feast". And off the soldiers wandered, down the road.

The story of the stone soup is a very old tale thats told all around the world. I included it here, not just because it's inspirational, but it highlights exactly what I believe is the process of going from idea to implementation. The soldiers start with nothing more than a stone (an idea) and with the help of a great team, plenty of courage and passion and creativity they end up with a delicious pot of soup.

The contributions of the people in the village represent your financial backers, your resources, your team, etc. Each contribution that is made is adding up to the whole. Everyone is helping you to realise your goal and make a difference in the world with your idea.

GET YOUR IDEAS DOWN ON PAPER

A daily technique that I use to generate ideas I call the 90 minute Jam Session. Basically what I do is find somewhere quiet for 90 minutes where I can relax. I bring my notebook and a pen and I spend 90 minutes brainstorming or mind-mapping an idea that I am working on. I shut off all distractions for 90 minutes. I don't take any calls on my phone or check my email. For 90 minutes, I focus on this one task. It's always amazing how much I can get done and the ideas that come to mind in that 90 Minutes.

At the initial stage of coming up with your ideas, choose having a quantity of ideas over quality. Try and come up with as many ideas as you can. We will evaluate and filter out the ideas we are not going to work on later. In the idea discovery process it's important to let your ideas flow freely. Idea creation and idea evaluation are two very separate things. In a moment I will talk about idea evaluation, but for now lets focus on the idea creation part. Trying to both create and evaluate your ideas at the same time is like trying to talk and chew at the same time!

"The best way to have a good idea is to have a lot of ideas."

—Linus Pauling,
chemist, biochemist, peace activist, author, educator

Your ideas don't have to be original or brand new. You can build on the ideas of others. They can be something that's already been done that you put a new slant on and do in a different way. It may be a combination of two or more ideas that you have or have seen and bring together to create a completely different product. Remember, the day before something becomes a huge success it's just a crazy idea.

In Germany, 3 brothers known called the Samwer Brothers have made themselves very successful by cloning ideas. In the world of entrepreneurship innovation is celebrated, the Samwer's however are not originators, but they are extremely effective in their chosen field: they see concepts that are working in the US or Asia and replicate the approach for new markets with high barriers of entry. Their "clones" can be found in some of the large, non-English-speaking countries including Germany, China, Russia and Brazil.

There most successful cloning attempt was of the internet giant Ebay. The brothers say they sent several emails to eBay suggesting that the company establish an online auction platform in Germany, and that they should be hired to run it. When they didn't receive a reply, the brothers returned to Germany and, in January 1999, brought in three friends to develop their own platform. A month later they founded Alando — a German-language online auction website just like Ebay.

Among the first items for sale were their own childhood toys: Alex sold his train set, Marc auctioned an old pair of roller skates and Oliver some coins. The team also created what it called "category captains" who were each responsible for a specific area of the site. "We had one person focusing on stamp dealers, one person focusing on consumer electronics etc," Oliver says. "We took it into our own hands and didn't wait for the market to be founded." Within 100 days of going live, the site was sold to eBay for £35 million.

I share this example just to highlight that ideas are not always original. And they don't necessarily have to be.

"If you're going to think, think big". I love that quote by Donald Trump. If you follow what most of the mainstream media puts out today you will quickly see that there is a constant flow of negative news that gets pumped out all day long. The news companies are in the business of selling advertising and sponsorship and they know that alarming and negative news gets attention and in turn keeps the advertising revenue coming in. Negative news is their business. The downside is that, telling us how bad the world is causes people to be afraid of taking action to better their lives or to attempt to even change things for the better. It seems to me like all the negativity and talk of scarcity has taken a large part of our society into a psychological and spiritual recession.

A recession is " a period of temporary economic decline dining which trade and industrial activity are reduced". There are plenty of statistics to show that in times of financial recession, when there is an economic downturn, those who continue to make wise investments also make great financial rewards. In spite of all the negative news and the panic that ensues, these individuals recognise recession as a time of opportunity. A time of growth and expansion.

Wise entrepreneurs recognises that even when their seems to be a spiritual or psychological recession in society; where people have become apathetic and hopeless, it is also a time of great opportunity. It's not for you as an aspiring entrepreneur to get caught up in all of the negative news. Rather it's a time to be bold and courageous and to do something big and significant that will change the world.

I want to challenge and encourage you to take on issues and problems that will make a big difference in the world. Dare to dream big and to make an attempt to solve some of the worlds biggest problems. Technology and the Internet makes it increasingly possible for you to do that now.

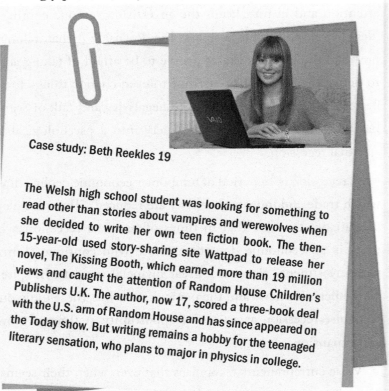

Case study: Beth Reekles 19

The Welsh high school student was looking for something to read other than stories about vampires and werewolves when she decided to write her own teen fiction book. The then-15-year-old used story-sharing site Wattpad to release her novel, The Kissing Booth, which earned more than 19 million views and caught the attention of Random House Children's Publishers U.K. The author, now 17, scored a three-book deal with the U.S. arm of Random House and has since appeared on the Today show. But writing remains a hobby for the teenaged literary sensation, who plans to major in physics in college.

"The future is here, it's just not evenly distributed"

A few years ago it would have been thought impossible for humans to fly out into space and land space craft on asteroids and mine the asteroids for precious metals as <u>Planetary Resources</u> are doing now. Neither would it have been thought possible for driverless electric cars to actually be on our roads. Already several states have passed laws for driverless cars to be on the roads.

Companies like Mercedes, Volvo, Audi, Apple, and Google are leading the way to get the cars on the roads.

Someone had the audacity to believe that it would be possible to create a 3D printer that can print actual human tissue, cars, houses, human limbs.Marc Goodman recently did a Ted Talk in which he presented 3D printed an actual gun <u>live on stage</u>. I just want you to stretch your thinking a little about what's possible.

A PROCESS FOR GETTING YOU IDEAS OUT OF YOUR HEAD AND ONTO PAPER

As I mentioned earlier, each morning I set aside time for what I call my 'Jam session'. This is the most important part of my day. This is when I get most of my productive work done. In my Jam session I usually start with the question , "How might I...?" Or "How can we...?" If its a financial goal I'm working towards I might say "How can I earn an extra £5000 this month?" I will make this the centre of my mind map and spend 90 minutes coming up with ideas and ways that I might be able to do that.

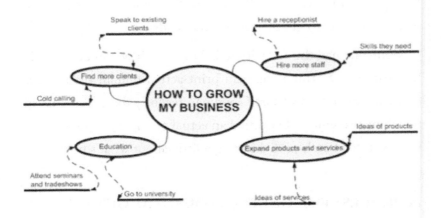

A CHALLENGE FOR YOU

I hope that by this point you have identified a goal or an idea that you want to develop. If you haven't got one yet, decide on a goal you want to achieve; whether it's a financial goal, a specific lifestyle or business goal, and conduct your own 90 minute Jam Session. This will enable you come up with an idea or goal that you can focus on in this next section. Please take a time out here to clarify your goals and come back to this point when you're done.

Ok. Now you have identified your idea, let's get practical. Here's what I want you to do. I want you to get a pen and paper out and write down one idea that you want to focus on. It doesn't have to be an essay, just a couple of sentences that explain the idea. For example, "My idea is to start a furniture recycling business: I want to take old office furniture that companies are throwing away. I want to repair it and restore it and make it available to others for sale via eBay." That is an example of a how you might write your idea.

Then write down the names of three people who can help you to achieve that goal or make that idea a reality andwrite down what it is exactly that you think they could help you do. In the case of the example of the furniture recycling idea, your three people might be

i.   The owner of a local furniture restoration company. Aim: To find out what the costs involved with restoring furniture are. What the industry is like. Whether there is a gap in the market for your idea. Whether there is a demand for reconditioned office furniture.

ii. A family friend that sells stuff on eBay: Aim: Find out how online selling works. Have they come across anyone doing what you're thinking about? What are the costs involved? What equipment might you need?

iii. A local office furniture removal company. Aim: To find out what happens to the furniture when they take it away. What costs are involved? How you can get a hold of some of the furniture. The barriers and challenges you will need to overcome. (Put this in a chart)

That should hopefully give you an idea of the type of people you need to be thinking about in relation to your idea. Remember, this is all about getting started, building up some momentum, getting that idea off the ground. While you're doing this, it's quite natural for limiting beliefs and thoughts to niggle in the back of your mind and try to hold you back. That's normal. You have to keep going. Make the calls, contact the people. Get as much information as you can. Based on the information you get from each person, make three more calls, then make three more and so on. What will happen is, either you will hit great success, or you will realise that actually the idea isn't one that is going to work. Again take a pause here to complete the task and come back when you're done.

Case study: Jamal Edwards

London based Jamal Edwards is building his own media empire. When he was 15 years old, he took a video camera and began filming his friends rapping on the streets of London. He uploaded the videos to his YouTube channel in 2007. The videos got enough hits to turn it into a business. He earned money from YouTube revenue for ads embedded in the videos.

He's worked with some of the biggest names in the music industry such as Nicki Minaj, Drake and Jessie J. His business, SB.TV is the UK's leading online youth broadcaster. He's an ambassador for the Prince's Trust and in 2013 he signed a deal with Sony RCA to have his own record label.

Hot Tip #1: You can earn advertising revenue from online platforms like YouTube and successful websites, if you can get enough visitors.

Hot Tip #2: That good idea that you are looking for could be a hobby or activity you already do. It could be sitting right in front of your face.

Ok great. At this point you have either discovered that your idea is a goer or it needs to go for a rethink. If it needs a rethink, simply go back and do another 90 minute Jam session and see what comes up. Where you go for those Jam sessions are really important too. Environment is important. Try and go somewhere inspirational where you can focus. If you're working as part of team, then its ok to bring your team with you.

Google CEO Larry Page said this about the idea development process, "We always try to concentrate on the long term. Many of the things we started— like (Google) Chrome— were seen as crazy when we launched them. So how do we decide what to do? How do we decide what's really important to work on? I like to call it the "toothbrush test." The toothbrush test is simple: Do you use it as often as you use your toothbrush? For most people, I guess that's twice a day. I think we really want things like that. We use Gmail much more than twice a day. And YouTube. Those things are amazing. Our philosophy is that the things that people use often are really important to them and we think that over time, you can make money from those things." (Source Bold Book, P. Diamandes 2015)

If the idea is good to go there's still a bit more to do before we go and start making products. So, from your initial conversations you may have identified that there is a niche in the market for what you are offering; maybe no one else is doing it and people have suggested they would be willing to pay for it. Maybe its already being done but you see a unique handle from which you can approach it.

The next important thing to do, which will save you time and money is to market your product before you actually create it. It's good to know if people want what you have to offer before you put a lot of work into making it. One way you can do this is by sending out surveys to potential customers and getting an idea if they would buy it and what they would be willing to pay for it. Or there's another way.

When I was just kicking off my school speaking business I only had a couple of schools that I had delivered programmes in. A friend of mine was a coordinator for a group of schools in the north of the city. I had mentioned to her about some of the work I was doing in one school and shared some evaluations with her. She was quite impressed and invited me to come and pitch my leadership programme to the groups of schools that she was meeting with. If they liked my work, as a team they would buy the programs off me in bulk. This was a big deal for me.

The only problem was that at that time I didn't actually have any programmes. All I had was the structure of the programme. The weekly themes, the topics that I would be covering, how I would evaluate the programme and provide feedback. I created a 3-4 minute video with some help from a friend from church, and went to the meeting and showed them the video. The video had snippets from some other workshops I'd done previously, lots of photos and me talking into the camera. I was amazed that 5 of the schools said yes, they would like me to come and deliver my programme in their schools.

Now that I had sold the product in advance, I then went away and actually created the course content. I marketed the product before I created it, as we saw in the last chapter— but if you're adventurous, you can also just put something out there, see what the response is, and then figure out how to make it.

In Chris Guillebeau's book, $100 Start Up, I read of a man that did this with an information product aimed at the high-end car industry. The story goes:

"He offered a specialty guide that sold for $900...except he didn't actually create it before he advertised it in a magazine. He knew it would be a lot of work to put together the guide, so why do the work if no one wanted it? Partly to his surprise, he received two orders. The cost of the ad was just $300, so that represented a $1,500 profit, if he could actually create the guide. He wrote to the two buyers and said he was developing a new and improved "2.0 version" of the guide and would love to send it to them at no additional charge as long as they could wait thirty days for it to be finished. Of course, he offered to refund their money if they didn't want to wait, but both buyers chose to wait for the 2.0 version. He then spent the next month frantically writing the guide before sending it to the eagerly waiting customers. Since he knew he had a success on his hands (and it helped that he actually had a product now), he placed another ad and sold ten more over the next few months."

Maybe you will take a different approach but the key thing is to make sure there is sufficient demand for your product or service before spending your whole life working on it. That's why it's so important to get started as quickly as possible and why the first sale can be so empowering.

A low cost way to test your idea today is by using Facebook advertising. Through Facebook advertising you can target your ideal customers wherever they are in the world. I recommend you read Perry Marshall's book on Facebook Advertising for a more in depth guide. You can get it <u>here.</u>

Once you've figured out that people want what you're offering, you need to raise some money to help you get started and to create a website and come up with a means for you to receive money.

In the next chapter I'll talk about how you can raise some money to get your idea off the ground.

ACTION:

1. Ideas are Everywhere.

The trick is being able to develop our minds so that we are able to spot them. Clearing your mind and allowing your imagination to flow is crucial to coming up with, and developing new ideas.

Have a look at the way the 'Google'organisation operates and see what you can learn from them about creatively and using the power of your imagination.

2. There's no such thing as a new idea. There's no such thing as a bad idea!

Your ideas don't have to be original or brand new, you can combine several different ideas or even build on the ideas of others. The big thing you have in your favour is that most people don't follow through with their ideas!

Small tweaks and changes to products and services can have enormous impact and help you build a successful business.

"There is no such thing as a new idea ..... We simply take a lot of old ideas and put them into a sort of mental kaleidoscope. We give them a turn and they make new and curious combinations. We keep on turning and making new combinations indefinitely .... Mark Twain

3. The process of creating ideas and the process of evaluating ideas are two very separate things.

To begin, focus on quantity. Here are a couple of things you can do:

- carry a notebook with you everywhere / create an ideas note in your phone – jot down ideas as they come into your head – when you see something, whilst you're talking to someone – note them or lose them;

- your mind works best when it is relaxed and focused – take yourself to somewhere quiet where you won't be interrupted, switch your phone off and clear you mind and mind-map all the ideas that come into your head.

Then start evaluating (whilst adding to your ideas)

Take a helicopter view and link ideas that are linked.

First instinct – then logic.

Decide which ideas you feel are worth pursuing – then start to do your homework on exploring those ideas from a business perspective.

"The best way to have a good idea is to have lots of ideas" Linus Pauling, Chemist, peace activist, author.

"There's no such thing as a bad idea, ... It has really helped us sort of really be creative and different. And I think that's what drives our business." Alex Fisher (Stelco)

4. Commitment is important in the process of creating and developing ideas. Many people don't notice their ideas and continue on the established, safe path.

Some of our best ideas come during those times when we are forced to act or respond to a challenge.

Challenge yourself to look round and ask yourself questions to prompt ideas:

- What am I really interested in?
- What could I improve?
- How can I help solve that challenge?
- What am I really good at?
- Who do I know who can help me?
- How can I collaborate?
- How do I want to make a difference?

CHAPTER 7

Raising the money you need to get your idea off the ground

"Nothing can stop the man with the right mental attitude from achieving his goal; nothing on earth can help the man with the wrong mental attitude".

I was speaking to a teenager earlier this week about starting up her own business. This young person is seriously talented. She's the creative, fun type, that people like to hang around with. As we got talking about her idea of starting up her own music recording studio, she began to speak about the kind of music she would like to record for herself and for other artists. It was clear it would be a dream come true for her if this idea could be developed.

I asked her what was stopping her and she said matter of factly "MONEY!" I said, "What about money? Whats money done to you?" "I don't have any!", she said.

It's fair to say that she didn't come from the wealthiest of families and any requests to parents for money to buy equipment were met with a firm and resounding no! Not having any cash meant she couldn't purchase the equipment that she needed to develop her idea and get it off the ground and so she felt stuck and a little hopeless.

From what I could tell, the problem wasn't so much that she didn't have any money; the problem was that she couldn't see any possible way to raise the money or to get the equipment she needed. This is a problem for a lot of young entrepreneurs.

A recent study by the Kaufmann foundation highlighted that most young people identify their biggest barrier to starting a business as raising finance. The challenge that my young friend was facing in trying to raise funds for studio equipment is clearly a big challenge for a lot of young people today.

WHERE THERE IS A WILL THERE IS A WAY

You simply cannot allow the lack of finances to stop you from getting your idea or business off the ground. You have got to get creative and think outside the box. When you have the desire and commitment and are willing to step out of your comfort zone you will find a way. You have to have a 'I'll do whatever it takes' attitude.

Just as an example for you, my first book "From the Postcode to the Globe" was self published in 2012. Now, I had the benefit of having a UK based publishing company agree to publish my book for me. What this meant was that I would get some support with the editing, they would help to market and promote the book and sell as many books as possible.

About 6 months before the proposed publishing date I received a phone call from the publisher to say that, unfortunately, they were declaring themselves bankrupt. They had run out of money and they would no longer be able to support my book project.

At the time, I had very little personal funds to get the book completed and marketed. I didn't know what to do. I was left with the text and the artwork for the book and that was it. As far as I was concerned, I had come too far to give up. I had put so much time and work into writing the book, some way, some how this book had to come to print.

I remember listening to an audio recording by one of my mentors Mike Murdoch. He has written and published hundreds of books. He talked about how to raise finance for your book. He suggested the idea of writing a letter to all the people you know telling them about your project and asking them to make a small investment. I thought it was a bold and slightly uncomfortable option but I had nothing else to lose.

So I wrote a one page letter. In the letter I outlined my writing journey, the reason for writing the book, what had happened with my publisher, and the support that I needed to get the project completed. I requested that each person consider putting £50 towards the project.

I was amazed at the response. Every single person that I address the letter to respond positively. Some even gave more than £50. When all the money came in I eventually had more than enough to get the book completed, to get copies printed up and to start the marketing campaign. I was blessed. It was a lot of work, but it was well worth it.

That book has gone on to sell several thousands of copies and touch the lives of people all around the world. If you haven't read it yet you should check it out on Amazon.

Asking friends and family to support your idea is just one of the ways you can generate the funds you need to get you idea off the ground. There are several other creative ways you can generate income to get your idea off the ground. Here are some other ideas and examples for you.

• **Use your savings**

If you have managed to save any money that you have been given as pocket money or spending money from parents you can begin to put some of that money towards developing your business idea.

• **Crowdfunding**

Crowdfunding is the practice of funding a project or venture by raising many small amounts of money from a large number of people, typically via the internet. Some of the most popular crowd funding platforms are _www.kickstarter.org_, _www.indiegogo.com_ and _www.wefund.com_. If you are under 18, you will require parental consent to use theses types of platforms. Here's a couple of examples of successful teen crowdfunding campaigns.

Case Study: Laurence Rook, UK

A 13-year-old boy from south London has invented a doorbell which calls the householder if nobody answers the door.

Laurence Rook, from Croydon, said he got thinking about his invention after his mother missed several deliveries.

The doorbell, with a built-in Sim card and an intercom, calls the householder if no-one answers the door within eight seconds, allowing the visitor to speak directly to the householder.

Laurence has already received orders worth up to £250,000 for the product.

A Dragons' Den-style competition at his school, the Trinity School, led to him developing his idea further - but he could not enter the competition as his working prototype was not ready in time.

Laurence, from Whyteleafe, said: "It started over a year ago when my mum was expecting a parcel to be delivered.

"It was the second or third delivery, and instead of leaving a slip saying 'please come to this post office and collect your parcel,' I thought, 'why don't they call you?'

"And from there I thought of the idea of putting a phone inside the doorbell so you can talk to them.

"We have got orders from a company called Commtel Innovate and they have ordered 20,000 units and another company that is thinking of ordering 25,000 units."

Laurence has received orders of £250,000

On his plans for the profits, he said: "I would like to put some of it away for university and future things I might like to do, and then the other half I'd treat myself - clothes, games, everything I can."

Family friend Paula Ward, also an inventor, helped Laurence.

She said: "I worked with him from his basic drawings and how he wanted it to work.

"I got in touch with my contacts over in the Far East and got them to build prototypes."

Laurence's mother Margaret Rook said: "We are very proud of Laurence. It's been an exciting week."

The doorbell could be available in High Street stores as soon as September.

Source: www.bbc.co.uk

'While most 11-year-olds are watching Hunger Games or doing other typically pre-teen things, Lily Born, of Chicago, is busy designing unbreakable, un-spillable kitchenware to help people with Parkinson's disease. She raised over $60,000 in a Kickstarter crowdfunding campaign to develop the product.'

'16-Year-Old Raises Over $20,000 In Crowdfunding for Nancy Drew Board Game

Strong, resourceful, and smart, Nancy Drew is a timeless role model. The Nancy Drew Board Game is a continuation of the beloved book series, meant to celebrate, and educate kids about, one of literature's most empowering characters.

Quincy MacShane is the creator of the Nancy Drew Board Game. Nancy Drew has been an inspiration to her and she feels the character can be an inspiration to other kids as well. Quincy designed this trivia board game as a fun way for new generations to learn about Nancy Drew and the power of reading.'

'Teen Raises Over $300K Through Crowdfunding To Help Man Who Walks 21 Miles A Day To Work

James Robertson has been walking 21 miles, without complaint, to his factory job. The commute left him time for only about two hours of sleep per night. And, in 10 years of walking to work after his old car died, he never missed a day of work. When 19-year-old Evan Leedy, a student at Detroit's Wayne State University, got wind of Robertson's ordeal, he started a GoFundMe campaign hoping to raise $5,000 to buy him a beater.'

- **Sell things on platforms like eBay**

Jamie Dunn from the UK started out at age 15 selling his parents old CD's and his old computer games on a market stall in the West Midlands, UK. He has gone on to be a successful entrepreneur since then. Do you have any things at your house that you can sell online and convert into cash? Make sure to get permission first, but you might find that there is a source of income to start your business right there where you are.

- **Get a part time job or do odd jobs**

As a teenager, I washed cars, I did a paper round and I worked on my uncles market stall to earn a bit of extra cash. I needed to earn myself some extra spending money, so that I could go out with my friends and have money to spend. In most countries when you are above the age of 13 you can go and get some part-time work to help to generate income to help you develop your idea or project.

- **Approach local businesses for sponsorship**

I was astounded at the response I received from local businesses when I was starting my first project. It was a social enterprise designed to give inner city young people the opportunity to express their talents and get recognised. The aim was to hold a high-profile event that would give the young people a platform. The first thing we did was approach the owner manager of one of the biggest and best hotels in town and ask them to give us the place for free. He said, yes. We had a free venue. We then contacted local clothes shops, shoe shops, hair and beauty companies, celebrities, and got them all involved. They all donated their time or their products and services to help us to make the event a success. All we had to do is have the courage to make the BIG ASK. To go out and ask people for help. Who do you know right now that has the resources or the cash that you need that you could make the BIG ASK to? Don't delay go out and ask the question.

Case study: Teen Bamboo Bike Manufacturer from Ghana

At 15 years old, Winnifred Shelby co-founded Ghana Bamboo Bikes Initiative in an effort to address unemployment and environment degradation through effective use of local resources. Now 19, Winnifred can boast of producing 60 to 100 bicycles a month, employing 10 employees with an average family of 5 (most of them women). Winnifred is a finalist in one of Africa's most prestigious awards for young entrepreneurs -- the Anzisha prize. Her company, Ghana Bamboo, is recognised for being environmentally friendly and sustainable with local resources. On her website she says:

"The Ghana Bamboo Bikes is a socio-ecological green initiative that addresses the quadruple problems of climate change, poverty, rural-urban migration and high unemployment amongst the youth in rural Ghana by creating employment opportunities and sustainable livelihood job skills for the youth through the building of high quality handcrafted second generation bamboo bikes for the international export markets. "We also manufacture multipurpose second generation bamboo bikes that are suitable for the high terrain and rough roads and purposeful for the local needs using native bamboo.

"We believe that business opportunities exists in all the areas of Ghana and are committed to improving the standard of living of young Ghanaians through the creation of sustainable social enterprises.

"We are committed to promoting fair trade, treating people fairly, profit sharing with builders, creating environmentally responsible products that contribute in reducing climate change commitment to protect the environment and promoting environmental awareness."

- **Look for a partner or investor that has the funds that you need.**

Perhaps you don't have the cash right now but somebody else you know does have it. Consider the idea of pitching your idea to them with the view to them giving you the cash amount you need to get our business started in return for a share in the business. They might give you £x for x% stake in your profits.

- **Secure grants form public or private organisations**

When I was starting the social enterprise that I mentioned earlier, I was fortunate to be able to secure some grant funding from the local council. The funding helped me to pay for the marketing and promotional costs as well as other running costs for the event. There are usually similar grant funding schemes available in most major cities in the world. If none are available near you then have a look online at *www.teenbusiness.com* for some inspiration.

ACTION:

Here are 7 ways you can raise money to help start your business:

1. Friends and Family

Friends and family may support your idea and contribute to, or help generate, the funds you need to get your idea off the ground. This is often useful for a small amount of start-up money to support things such as piloting service or making prototypes of products

This can be a loan or for a percentage of your business by those who are interested in investing becoming shareholders. This can also be linked to you getting practical advice, support and mentoring from family and friends with relevant experience.

2. Crowd Funding

Crowd funding platforms like Indiegogo, Kickstarter and Gofundme are a way you can obtain funding by small contributions from a large number of people committed to your idea. Crowd funding is more usually a source of funding for social enterprises – those businesses whose work has social value. It works best for very specific ideas and good stories.

There is a lot of advice for the best way to approach crowd funding and key steps to take to give you the best chance of success.

3. Sell – Sell – Sell!

You can have the best products and services in the world but they are of no value for anyone unless you can sell them! Practicing selling is helpful for any entrepreneur. You can raise funds for your business by selling goods in person or on-line e.g. on eBay. You could source something that you know people will buy – buy it at wholesale price and sell it at a retail price. I know a young man who made a very good living to fund his way through University selling baseball caps from a source in China. You are providing a service by sourcing something people want and making the all-important profit you need to start your business. There is a lot of advice you can find about setting-up and selling on e-bay.

4. Get a part-time job

There are many advantages of part-time work and even Nobel Winning Physicist, Richard Feynman talked about what he learned from working part-time in a hotel; whilst at school.

- You can learn lots from any business or organisation you work.
- It's different to study
- Whilst you're working you're not spending

5. Sponsorship

As a way of raising funds you could approach local businesses / organisations for sponsorship. Ensure there are benefits for the business / organisation that you approach. This can also be linked to getting practical advice, support and mentoring from business people with relevant experience.

6. Partner – Investor

There may be someone you could partner that has funds that could be invested in the business.

Business Angels and other investors are always looking for opportunities to invest in good ideas. Put your proposal together and share it with people who can help you to improve it.

7. Bid for Grants

Many organisations, public and private, provide opportunities for you to bid for funding to develop projects and business ideas. Look at local opportunities for you to access grants and get advice from those with experience of bidding for grants.

CHAPTER 8

How you can create and profit from your own information product in 7 days

"Move fast and break things. Unless you are breaking stuff, you are not moving fast enough".

—Mark Zuckerberg

To help you to see how simple it is to take an idea from the concept stage to implementation in this day and age, I'm going to guide you through a step-by-step process of creating a digital product that can be sold online. If you follow this procedure well, you can be in business and have products selling on line in the next 7 days.

These same principles can be applied to a whole range of different ideas and products. Think outside the box and use these principles help you to develop any kind of business that you have.

WHY A DIGITAL PRODUCT?

The number one reason why I'm choosing a digital product is because this is something I have personally done myself with my first book. I understand how it works from experience. Digital products can come in the form of online video, audio, ebooks, online courses, PDF's or a combination of all of the above. Digital products cost very little to produce, so you will have little or no costs to get started. It will be easy for you to market them via your social networks and using online tools. I want you to actually create something and put it out there. The type of product we are going to create is an ebook, but the process can be applied to any of the above digital products.

Step 1–Who is your customer?

Ok, let's begin. Your first task is to decide which audience or group of people you want to sell your product to. What age range are they? Where are they from? Are they male or female? What are they currently doing? Where might you meet them? Take 5-10 minutes to think about the ideal end user of your product. This should be someone that you can identify with. After completing this step you should have written down a brief description of your ideal end user. It might look like:

"My ideal product end user is an 18 year student, just starting university who lives in the UK".

Or, "Middle-class single parents living in central London earning above £100,000 per year."

Or "6th form students living in the UK, thinking of studying abroad for university"

Try and be as clear as you can about the end user that you want to target with your new digital product. Take 5-10 minutes and then come back here. Check out this blog post here on "How to identify your 'Avatar'" to help you get some more clarity. Don't go to step two until you've figured it out.

STEP 2: REFINE YOUR TARGET AUDIENCE

Ok, welcome back. Now you have your desired end user written down I'd like to challenge you to take it a little further. Take a look at your end user and break it down a little more specifically. Let's say you said your end user was "16 year old boys that enjoy watching football". I would want you to get even more detailed and say something like "16 year old boys from London that live in Hackney and like watching Liverpool FC, but have never been to watch them play live". This might seem like it's a little too detailed but it's very important. What you are doing is focusing your product on a specific piece of the market. The clearer you are about your market segment, the easier it is for you to focus your marketing strategy to be able to reach them with your product.

Keep it realistic though. Say, if your answer to question 1 was something like "females aged 18-30 interested in clothing", your new and more detailed version might be "females in the UK aged 18-30 interested in African wear made in West Africa."

Can you see the trend here? You want to get as specific as you can about your target customer or Avatar. This will be the 'niche' that your business will operate in. Take another 10 minutes or so to get some more clarity and then we'll continue.

STEP 3–TAKE A LOOK AT WHAT OTHERS ARE DOING IN THAT NICHE

Great, now you have come up with your target audience you're ready for your next task. Make sure you have completed the previous steps before going any further.

Go to *www.amazon.co.uk* and search for 'best sellers' in the search.

Search through the list of best sellers to find the top-ten titles that are targeted at your desired target reader. Or to your particular niche. They must be best sellers. Choose the top-ten titles that grab your attention the most. The ones that you find most appealing, that grab you emotionally or are the most interesting. Keep searching through. I want you to get your product completed as soon as possible, so try not to take any longer than 30 minutes to do this.

Again, don't read past here until your list is done. Go for it.

STEP 4–IDENTIFY WHAT THE BENEFITS WILL BE TO YOUR CUSTOMER FOR CHOOSING YOU OVER THE REST

Ok, so now that stage 3 is completed we need to identify what the benefits are to your audience for having used or read your product. So, they have downloaded it, what are the advantages to them for having purchased your product? What difference will it have made to their lives? What will they get out of it?

Many years ago I had a job selling advertising at the Birmingham Post and Mail Newspaper company. In our training they went to lengths to tell us the difference between 'selling points' and 'benefits'.

An example of a selling point is that "we make world class tyres". An example of a benefit is, "Our tyres are puncture proof and they last twice as long as our competitors."

or

Feature–"Our airplane seats have twice as much legroom as our nearest competitors"

Benefit–"We offer our passengers a much more comfortable, spacious and relaxed journey on their long haul flights."

A feature is descriptive, it's a characteristic of a product.

A benefit is emotional, it explains what the customer has to gain by using the product.

It's easier to make a list of features than it is to turn each of the features into benefits.

I always remember being told in our training that "people don't buy features they buy benefits".

List down what you think are the top 10 benefits for your product. Take another 30 minutes or so. You might want to take a break and come back to it tomorrow. If you're super pumped about getting this exercise done, do it as soon as possible. List your top 10 product benefits to the reader or user of your product.

Great, we're getting closer to the finish. Go back through your list of benefits and rank them from 1-10. Your number one benefit is the one that resonates most with you. Put a star by it, underline it, highlight it in some way.

You're doing great; you've come a long way already. Let's keep moving forward.

Your number one benefit is likely to be the one that deeply resonates with you most of all. This is the number one benefit to the reader of your book. This has to be clear, powerful and real.

The benefit must not leave the reader foggy about what you are offering. Take 30-60 minutes to go over this process and make sure you are clear about your No 1 benefit.

STEP 5–CREATE A LIST OF POSSIBLE TITLES

Ok, cool, now we are going to create a title for your book. The name of your product has to be catchy and easy to remember. You need to use credible and powerful words.

Go back to your list of 10 bestsellers that you found on Amazon. Look through those titles, they will hopefully get some ideas flowing.

Then find a quiet space, put on some relaxing music and take some time to write down as many possible titles for your product as you possibly can; at least 15 if not more. You can log on to Youtube and look for music to listen to while your working.

Time yourself, try and do this list in 20 minutes. Once you have created your list of 15 possible titles come straight back here and we'll go to the next step.

Try not to make your name too long and also ensure your number 1 benefit is clearly in your title.

STEP 6–SHORTLIST YOUR TITLES

Ok, well done again. You're moving closer to creating your first product. You should now have a list of upwards of 15 names. I'm going to challenge you now to whittle that list of names down to your top 5. Yes, 5. I know it might not be say to do, but you can do it.

Go through your list and choose the top 5 names that you think are catchy, powerful and will create an emotion in your reader and get the nature of the benefits across to potential readers.

STEP 7–TEST YOUR TITLE AND START GETTING THE 'COMMUNITY' INVOLVED

Now you need to do a little market research on your title idea, Go to *www.surveymonkey.com* and create an account for free. You're going to create a survey in which you will ask some people to look at your titles and rank them from 1-5 for you.

It's important to explain a little about your product in your survey. What exactly your niche is and the main benefit of the product to the reader. Providing this information will enable them to make a more informed choice. Its very straightforward to create a survey on Survey Monkey. The website allows you to share your survey via email or through social media. If you need help, check out their online tutorials or ask someone you know or contact the website directly.

The survey shouldn't take you more than 10 minutes to create and then you're going to contact your friends, family, social media networks and send them the link for the survey. Anyone you know. If you have people in your target audience you can send it to, that's great too. I think you need at least 20 responses. This should take no more than one day to get done. Go make a start on it. Get your survey done, put it out there and see what responses you get back. Do it as fast as you can.

Done? Awesome. Now it's decision time. You need to decide on your name. This name is going to be final. The time for gathering opinions is over. Trust in yourself, trust the process. Choose the name you're happy with and you believe is the one that's going to be most effective. Don't go any further without choosing THE NAME.

CHAPTER 9

Marketing and selling your product

"To be successful and grow your business and revenues, you must match the way you market your products with the way your prospects learn about and shop for your products". Brian Halligan.

Ok, so now you have the name for your digital ebook we are now going to the next step. Here's the formula we are going to use:

1.   Create the chapter headings

2.   Create content

3.   Market/Sell the product

Now, in some cases it's wiser to swap steps 2 and 3 around. To market the product before you create the content. I would recommend you do this if you're creating something other than a book. If you were creating an online video course for example. You would be able to create a one page website. An outline of the context and market it to see if anyone wanted it before you spent the time to create the product.

In the case of a book, we need to create some valuable content. This book is going to be a book that people will be able to read quickly.

STEP 1–CREATE CHAPTER HEADINGS

First we are going to create your chapter headings. Earlier you wrote down 10 benefits to your reader and you ranked them in order of importance. You have used the main benefit to create the title of your book, you have nine left. Those remaining benefits are going to be the chapters of your book.

Go back to the benefits and rewrite them as specifically as you can, in a way that connects the benefit to the end result. For example, instead of saying, "Develop a sense of humour", say "How to instantly put a smile on the face of everyone you meet."

Start as many of your titles you can with 'HOW'. Most people reading your type of book (Non-fiction) are looking to learn how to do something. How to get from A to B. It's human nature. People are looking for solutions to problems.

Sort them into a logical sequence for the reader. They should be able to read your chapter heading and see that there is a step by step process for them to follow. Do this exercise right now. Spend 30 minutes to 1 hour getting this done.

You've written your 9 chapter titles. You're probably thinking to yourself, "How am I going to create the content for each chapter?". We're going to keep this very simple. Remember, our aim is to help you get your first product available for sale.

STEP 2–CREATE CONTENT

Ok, lets create that content. Here's where we are going to start. Write a 2-3 page article under each chapter title. Write in the same way that you speak. Imagine you are writing to your target reader about that particular benefit. Explaining how they will get that result.

Type up your article into a word document or text file and convert them into a PDF document. Feel free to add images. Keep your paragraphs short so that it is easier for the reader to read. In each article give them 3 steps they need to take in order to arrive at their desired outcome and get the results that they want to achieve. Some people will do exactly what you've asked them to do. The aim is for them to achieve massive results and hopefully come back and give you great testimonials.

STEP 3–MARKET/SELL THE PRODUCT

Log on to *www.fiverr.com* and search for a designer for your book cover. You will get a good book cover designed for just $5. Once your book cover is designed and your content is ready to go you are almost ready to start selling. You need to decide what your selling price is going to be. Take a look at what similar books are selling for on Amazon Kindle and choose a competitive price. As its a relatively short read you don't want to price your book to high.

The Amazon Kindle platform is a simple way for you to begin to sell your books online. I recommend that you set up an

Amazon account and follow the tutorial on how to sell your book online. You may also want to sell your book on your own personal webpage. Search Youtube for video tutorials for how to create an online shop on your Wordpress site.

Selling your book online via your own website will mean that you get a greater percentage of the profit. Selling on Amazon or any other such site will mean that they take a cut from your profit. The upside to using Amazon or another online retailer is that you're able to leverage the Amazon brand and use some of their marketing tools to help promote your book.

My friend Amanda C. Watts is a marketing expert. This is what she says about how you can market and promote your product online.

How To Market Your Digital Products: eBooks, Videos, Mp3s and Podcasts by Amanda C. Watts, from http:// www. awakenyourmagic.com

Having assets for your business, in the form of digital products, allows customers to have access to your content 24 hours a day, 7 days a week.

Raising awareness of your digital products couldn't be easier— if you get the right foundations in place.

First: Know your client. It is imperative that the products you create are suitable for your ideal client and chosen niche. If you know your client, and where they hang out (online and offline) you can get in front of them—raising awareness and marketing your digital products, with ease.

Second: Know the benefits of your product. People won't buy the features (it's an eBook, video, MP3 etc.) but they will buy the solution your digital product gives them. Make sure your marketing is about the benefits the product delivers, not the product itself.

Third: Make is easy for customers to buy/download. A confused mind never buys; so don't have too many products for customers to choose from. Create products of HUGE value, invest time and your expertise in creating them, and have them sell with ease.

Here are key platforms to market your digital products on:

FREE

Social Media Networks: Post links to your digital products on Facebook Pages and Facebook Groups, Twitter, LinkedIn Groups and LinkedIn Updates, Instagram, Pinterest... invest time in a couple of platforms and build relationships with people, time is not infinite, so use it wisely.

Measure your return on these free updates by the number of downloads you have received from these platforms.

In Your Newsletter: As you grow your profile online, more people will want to join your mailing list. Make sure you include links to your digital products in your monthly/weekly newsletter. These people will have 'opted in' to hear from you, so they will have some trust in your offerings already.

Speaking Opportunities: The biggest and easiest way to grow your credibility is to speak in front of your ideal clients. Make sure that when you speak, the least you do is get everyone's email address. By getting their email address you can then market your digital products to them after the event. Alternatively, get them to buy your digital products immediately... it makes for an easy sale.

Amazon and iTunes: Upload your eBooks to Amazon, and your podcasts to iTunes. Easy to do, just follow their instructions.

Guest Blogs: Getting the opportunity to guest blog will raise your profile and show you as an expert in your unique genius. Sell your digital products at the end of the guest blogs, in your Authors Bio.

PAID

Advertising: Most of the social media networks enable you to have paid targeted advertising. Keep an eye on your return on investment, but LinkedIn, Facebook and Twitter are proving to be very successful for small and large business owners alike.

Google: Google Pay Per Click is still going strong. Again keep an eye on your Return On Investment, but getting it right can sell heaps of your products.

Affiliate Marketing: You will lose a percentage of your profit, however, if you can find other people who have the same clients as you, but are not competitors, then you can get them to sell your products on your behalf. You will reach mass audiences, and having someone endorse you will build your credibility.

As you can see there are many ways to share your digital products online. If you know your ideal client, and where they hang, you can get in front of them easily. Have a product that supplies HUGE value and overcomes your customers' pain and you will have HUGE success.

Remember the steps I have given you in this chapter can be used with pretty much any product. I sincerely wish you all the best on your entrepreneurial journey.

I would really appreciate hearing your stories of how you have been progressing on your Teenpreneur journey. Please drop an email to errol@errollawson.com and to share with me your success and your challenges. I'll do my best to help where I can. If it's ok with you I may even share your story in my next book.

PRAISE FOR TEENPRENEUR

"Your time is limited, so don't waste it living someone else's life. Hidden inside of you are treasures of talents, dreams, and innovative ideas that the world is yet to know. Don't let the awesome treasures inside you die. I have through this book and it's definitely a great start to helping you develop and nurture a great business idea. Even if you don't want to be an entrepreneur, Teenpreneur will help bring out the treasures in you because the lessons in here have been proven and tested by successful people in every country on the face of the earth."

—Dr. Kofi Osei-Kusi

Executive President, Osei-Kusi Foundation

"You'll find a lot of lore between the covers of this publication that will make you appear impressive to your colleagues. But don't be caught simply reading for bragging rights, read it for its useful contents and applicable concepts.

"Teenpreneur; how to build business in your teens" is a well written easy to read handbook for junior entrepreneurs crafted with an unmistakable charming simplicity. Errol's vast experience in youth coaching is palpable in his writing style and tales. He explores relevant stories to inspire your faith and ignite your passion and exposes refreshing strategies to equip you for take-off and survive turbulence.

Today, though the average age of the worlds top 10 billionaires according to Forbes Magazine, suggests you may have to be a septuagenarian to be wealthy, that statistic belies a certain sublime truth which a study of just the first three reveals. Bill

Gates now 59 years formed the Lakeside Programmers Group at 13years and sold his first computer software at age 17. 75 year old Carlos Slim bought his first shares in a Mexican bank at age 12 and Warren Buffet now 84 years, started selling at age 6 and bought his first investment at age 11. If ever there's a timeless message about wealth creation that cannot been preached enough it is 'The Power of Early".

This book is bound to cause a revolution: it is a must-read for every young person with a dream. Go ahead grab two, one for yourself and another for your bestie and birth the CEO in you."

—Dr. William Okyere–Frempong
CEO, The HuD Group Ghana &
Ag. Medical Superintendent LEKMA Polyclinic

RECOMMENDED READING LIST

$100 Start up–Chris Guillabeau

Entrepreneur Revolution–Daniel Priestley

The Slight Edge–Jeff Oslon

BOLD–Peter Diamandes

Starting - Andrew Priestley

Rich dad poor dad–Robert Kiyosaki

The suitcase entrepreneur–Nicola Sissons

The 7 Habits of Highly effective Teens - S. Covey

The richest man in Babylon - G. Clason

Think and Grow Rich - N. Hill

The Bible

From the Postcode to the Globe - E. Lawson The

E - Myth - M. Gerber

Awaken the giant within - A. Robbins

RECOMMENDED PODCASTS

Entrepreneur on fire - John Lee Dumas

The Tai Lopez Show - Tai Lopez

The School of greatness - Lewis Howes

10x talk - Joe Polish and Dan Sullivan

Eventual Millionaire - Jamie Tardy

The EntreLeadership Podcast - Dave Ramsey

The Smart Passive Income Podcast - Pat Flynn

Made in the USA
Middletown, DE
02 August 2023

36147657R00096